A Parent's Guide to Autism is must [...]
the autism spectrum. I learned a lot [...]
my social skills and become a better [...]
particularly helpful advice for relatives and friends of [...]
viduals on the spectrum on how to help them identify and
develop their special gifts and overcome their handicaps.
Ron's Christian pastoral touch beautifully illustrates Paul's
teaching in 2 Corinthians 4 about how all of us, neuro-
atypical and neurotypical, need to develop the humility and
grace to allow God's glory to shine through our apparent
deficiencies.

—DR. HUGH ROSS
ASTRONOMER AND PASTOR
PRESIDENT OF REASONS TO BELIEVE AND AUTHOR OF
SEVENTEEN BOOKS ON CREATION

If the world fears the diagnosis of *autism*, then Ron
Sandison's prescription helps us discover instead how those
across the autism spectrum are variously gifted instru-
ments of the Holy Spirit to accomplish God's redemptive
work in the world. This parent's guide thus is honest about
autism's challenges, but through such, it opens up windows
into unimagined possibilities for us all.

—DR. AMOS YONG
PROFESSOR OF THEOLOGY AND MISSIONS AT
FULLER THEOLOGICAL SEMINARY
AUTHOR, *THE BIBLE, DISABILITY, AND THE CHURCH:
A NEW VISION OF THE PEOPLE OF GOD*

Ron Sandison uses his own journey with Asperger's, his
"insider's" knowledge of the worlds of autism, and extensive research and conversations with professionals, families,
and people within those worlds to write a book to educate and encourage parents, families, and others seeking
to find and nurture the gifts in every person. Along the
way he also shares his evangelical Christian faith, his seminary training, and his spiritual discipline of memorizing

Bible verses to illuminate the journey. In fact, the reader can sense Ron's growth in confidence, honesty, sensitivity, and self-reflection as the book progresses. He thus joins a growing number of people with autism who are talking directly about their faith in the growing number of voices at the intersections of faith, theology, and disability.

—BILL GAVENTA, MDIV
DIRECTOR, SUMMER INSTITUTE ON
THEOLOGY AND DISABILITY

Brimming with insight and compassion, Ron Sandison is a wonderful storyteller. Just as Jesus used parables to teach lessons, Ron uses unforgettable stories to help convey important concepts and principles about autism. He weaves together his strong Christian faith and an understanding of his own autism with the stories of others on the autism spectrum. This book takes the reader to a new level of empathy and respect for individuals who live with autism.

—LINDA HODGDON, MED, CCC-SLP
INTERNATIONAL AUTISM CONSULTANT
AUTHOR OF THE BEST-SELLING BOOK
VISUAL STRATEGIES FOR IMPROVING COMMUNICATION

With autism spectrum disorder (ASD) on the rise, so are the number of published studies and personal accounts of the lives of those with autism. However, rarely do we find an author diagnosed with autism so clearly blend individual experiences with such proficient knowledge. Ron offers a perspective that contains current, accurate research within a theological framework. This sheds light on the vast struggles and significant issues we need to understand as we embrace those with differences. I applaud Ron for handling this complex subject clearly, authentically, and effectively.

—COLLEEN SWINDOLL-THOMPSON
SPECIAL-NEEDS MINISTRY DIRECTOR
INSIGHT FOR LIVING

If you are looking for an in-depth study to help you navigate the Christian response to autism, this book is for you. Ron has given a personal and professional perspective on the challenges of autism spectrum disorder and how we as believers can respond. He has come a long way in his own personal journey. Ron's unique insights will help readers understand how they can not only respond well, but also how they can overcome with God's help. I know that as you read this book, you will be encouraged and blessed.

—PASTOR CRAIG JOHNSON
DIRECTOR, MINISTRIES AT LAKEWOOD CHURCH
HOUSTON, TEXAS

Finally the world is starting to realize the many strengths and gifts that individuals with autism spectrum disorder can offer. Ron is a perfect example of the great intelligence we often see in those on the autism spectrum. His book is interesting, insightful, and intriguing. The challenges that he endured in his younger years are unbelievable, and his resilience is incredible. Ron's book is truly amazing. Every reader will appreciate his honest and captivating stories.

—LYNN KERN KOEGEL, PHD
DIRECTOR, KOEGEL AUTISM CENTER
UNIVERSITY OF CALIFORNIA–SANTA BARBARA

It's absolutely fantastic to know that books are being written by people with autism—demonstrating to the world how successful people on the autism spectrum can be. I especially appreciate Ron's unique slant encompassing spirituality and autism, since spirituality is very abstract and people on the spectrum are typically very literal and concrete. Being a deeply spiritual person, this is truly important to me. I believe it is also critical to the world, as more and more people can learn to have peace in their heart and be accepting of differences and the unique abilities of others. Kudos to you, Ron, for writing this book. Through your work you will certainly spread light in an area where darkness has prevailed in the past.

—KAREN SIMMONS SICOLI
FOUNDER AND CEO OF AUTISM TODAY
AND AN AWARD-WINNING AUTHOR

In this "one-of-a-kind" publication Ron Sandison shares his unique experience with autism, autism facts and science, and relevant Holy Scripture to provide a valuable resource for anyone who is interested in learning more about autism and how to support the autism spectrum disorder (ASD) community. As a professional in this field, I see individuals affected by autism. Because of their differences, both individuals and families feel rejected by society and churches. Reaching out to all affected by autism, whether it's an individual on the spectrum or families with autistic children, is of great importance. We must act in Christian love, as we are to be God's hands and feet, and seek those in need.

This book reveals practical insights on how one can take action to reach out to, and understand, people on the autism spectrum. However, I have yet to read a book with the kind of complete package contained in this one. This book is a true blessing to individuals with autism, their family members, teachers, neighbors, church leaders—really, it's for everyone!

—KIMBERLY ISAAC-EMERY, MS
AUTISM SPECIALIST
CERTIFIED RELATIONSHIP DEVELOPMENT
INTERVENTION CONSULTANT
WWW.AUTISMWITHEXCELLENCE.COM

A PARENT'S GUIDE TO
AUTISM

A PARENT'S GUIDE TO
AUTISM

RON SANDISON

SILOAM

Most CHARISMA HOUSE BOOK GROUP products are available at special quantity discounts for bulk purchase for sales promotions, premiums, fund-raising, and educational needs. For details, write Charisma House Book Group, 600 Rinehart Road, Lake Mary, Florida 32746, or telephone (407) 333-0600.

A PARENT'S GUIDE TO AUTISM by Ron Sandison
Published by Siloam
Charisma Media/Charisma House Book Group
600 Rinehart Road
Lake Mary, Florida 32746
www.charismahouse.com

This book or parts thereof may not be reproduced in any form, stored in a retrieval system, or transmitted in any form by any means—electronic, mechanical, photocopy, recording, or otherwise—without prior written permission of the publisher, except as provided by United States of America copyright law.

Unless otherwise noted, Scripture quotations are taken from the Holy Bible, New International Version®, NIV®. Copyright © 1973, 1978, 1984, 2011 by Biblica, Inc.™ Used by permission of Zondervan. All rights reserved worldwide. www.zondervan .com. The "NIV" and "New International Version" are trademarks registered in the United States Patent and Trademark Office by Biblica, Inc.™

Scripture quotations marked MEV are taken from the Holy Bible, Modern English Version. Copyright © 2014 by Military Bible Association. Used by permission. All rights reserved.

Scripture quotations marked THE MESSAGE are from *The Message: The Bible in Contemporary English*, copyright © 1993, 1994, 1995, 1996, 2000, 2001, 2002. Used by permission of NavPress Publishing Group.

Scripture quotations marked NKJV are taken from the New King James Version®. Copyright © 1982 by Thomas Nelson. Used by permission. All rights reserved.

Scripture quotations marked NLT are from the Holy Bible, New Living Translation, copyright © 1996, 2004, 2007. Used by permission of Tyndale House Publishers, Inc., Wheaton, IL 60189. All rights reserved.

Copyright © 2016 by Ron Sandison
All rights reserved

Cover design by Justin Evans

Visit the author's website at www.spectruminclusion.com.

Library of Congress Cataloging-in-Publication Data:
An application to register this book for cataloging has been submitted to the Library of Congress.
International Standard Book Number: 978-1-62998-671-5
E-book ISBN: 978-1-62998-672-2

Every effort has been made to ensure that the information contained in this book is complete and accurate. However, neither the publisher nor the author is engaged in rendering professional advice or services to the individual reader. The ideas, procedures, and suggestions contained in this book are not intended as a substitute for counseling with a professional who knows your child and is able to accurately assess if a program is accomplishing effective results. Every matter in regard to your child's health requires medical supervision from your child's pediatrician. Neither the author nor the publisher will be liable or responsible for any loss or damage allegedly arising from any information or suggestion in this writing.

The stories in this book are based on actual individuals with autism, but in some cases, names, and identifying characteristic have been altered.

First edition

16 17 18 19 20 — 987654321
Printed in the United States of America

I dedicate this book to my beautiful wife, Kristen Boswell Sandison, who loves me unconditionally. Proverbs 31:12 describes Kristen perfectly: "She brings him good, not harm, all the days of her life."

I also thank my parents, Chuck and Janet Sandison, who helped me overcome autism and follow the call of God; my brothers, Steve and Chuck, and their families; my sister-in-law, Heather, and her husband, Charlie; and my father- and mother-in-law, Bob and Suzanne Boswell, for letting me marry their beautiful daughter.

Lastly, I dedicate this work to my grandparents, Helen and Donald Olmsted, who published three books and wrote or directed more than one hundred murder-mystery plays, for inspiring me to be an author.

CONTENTS

ACKNOWLEDGMENTS

WOULD LIKE TO acknowledge those who helped make this book a reality, both with their precious time and investment in my life. I start with my agent, Les Stobbe, who continually encouraged me to keep the faith throughout the challenging writing process. Then, there is Pastor Rod Parsley, his wife, Joni, and their son, Austin, for their support with my book; David Harden for always believing in me; Sandra Woods Peoples for publishing my articles on her website, http://specialneedsparenting.net; and Dawn Escoto, for editing my manuscript for mechanics.

A special thanks to the authors and autism professionals who contributed short stories for the chapter "Stories From the Heart": Beth Aune, Lois Joan Brady, Jenny Thomas, Kathleen Bolduc, Craig Evans, Kelli Ra Anderson, and Dr. Lynn K. Koegel. Thanks also to Kristine Barnett for writing the foreword and for her many wonderful and inspiring words, and for April Vernon's poem, "Special-Needs Moms: A Look Inside."

Thanks to all the parents and professionals in the autism community whom I interviewed while writing this book. A special thanks also to Linda A. Hodgdon, Pastor Greg McDougall, Jill and Clay Marzo, Edie and Mikey Brannigan, Ray and Anthony Starego, Sandy and Robert Waters, Alexis Wineman, Kimberley Butterworth, Jas Dimitrion, William Stillman, Jeff Davidson, Dina Buno, Nikki Tomczak, Laurie Wallin, Jesse Saperstein, John Elder Robison, Toby Evans, Thomas Christianson, Scott Long, Timothy Welch, Dr. Bobby Newman, Dr. Peter Jensen, Rhonda Gelstein, Anthony Ianni,

Katie Celis, Grant and Julie M. Coy, Patty Myers, Melanie Fowler, Gary Mayerson, Lisa Simmons, Karen Simmons, Bill Davis, Michael John Carley, Heather Rogero, Lori Unumb, Susan Wood, Susan Osborne, Kimberly A. Isaac, Heidi Carabine, Mark Youngkin, Robin Hansen, Karen Trinkaus, Kelly Langston, Dr. Kurt Woeller, Pastor Craig Johnson, Lisa Jo Rudy, Dr. Stephen Mark Shore, Sean Barron, Brian King, Laura Corby, Colleen S. Thompson, Linda Young, Kristi Aycox, Dr. Michael D. Powers, Julie A. Reed, Dr. Margaret Bauman, Dr. Joanne Ruthsatz, Dr. Tony Attwood, Jacob Barnett, Wayne and Jennifer Gilpin, Dr. Fred R. Volkmar, Dr. Simon Baren-Cohen, Dr. Temple Grandin, and the countless others who contributed to this book.

I would like to thank my students at Destiny School of Ministry, and especially Pastor Lee and Dr. Yvonne Matlock, under whose leadership I have taught for the past ten years; they have demonstrated the true heart of a pastor. I also thank Debi Clements for her writing and editing skills.

My thanks to the team at Charisma House for their continual encouragement and desire to advance the gospel of Christ: Steve Strang, Debbie Marrie, Tessie Guell DeVore, Althea Thompson, Ann Mulchan, Jevon Bolden, Jason McMullen, Marcos Perez, Woodley Auguste, and Adrienne Gaines.

Finally, I would like to thank my family, coworkers, and friends for their encouragement on my writing journey. Above all, I must give credit to Jesus Christ for giving me the strength and grace to finish this book.

FOREWORD

ACCORDING TO LEARNING disabilities professionals and autism experts, this book could not be written. Yet it was. I met the author while searching around the world for something: a gift in the human spirit so rare that many once thought it scientifically impossible. I was trying to prove not only did it exist, but also the capacity for it existed within all of us. When this gift appears, it is a light to everyone who sees it. I sought to find courage that confounds even the medical community, research data, and public perceptions. I found that spirit in Ron.

When he was a child, doctors diagnosed Ron as having autism. They told Ron's mother he would never succeed in academics and sports or "lead a typical life." Nevertheless, we are about to sit down on buses on the way to a busy day at the office with paper cups of coffee, or in our homes at nightfall sipping steamy mugs of tea, with his words before us. Regardless of the venue, take time to mentally kick off your work shoes and listen. This is the story only lifetimes can tell.

It started in the year 2000, when my own son, Jacob, was also diagnosed with autism. He was not alone. Ron's mom and I, along with countless others in communities around the world, all sat down to a similar doctor's appointment. As the rates of diagnosis of autism soared, numerous parents seated in vinyl or plastic chairs, with restless toddlers in tow, received the same look—the slow breathing a doctor gives before he says the word: "Autism."

It is a common misconception that once a child is diagnosed, that moment in the doctor's office will go away. It was one bad appointment, and you can move on from that point. But it does not vanish. Moving on is nearly impossible. Preconceived notions and judgments about autism are everywhere. Autism is the reason for every behavior your child had before that moment and explains every behavior after it. From then on, it will be the first word on the minds of every teacher, therapist, friend, or grocery store clerk that your child will encounter.

Autism is defined as a pervasive developmental disorder, one that will affect everything from motor skills to speech to friendship to the ability to buy a candy bar at the local store or wear a pair of lace-up shoes. For those with autism, the word that comes to mind for all of these situations and more of the beautiful ones in life—like falling in love, riding a bike, driving a car, sharing a conversation with a friend over coffee, and working at a job you love—is *can't*.

We face the fear of the impossible, ranging from one failed Little League tryout to the next: canceled play dates, missed kindergarten-circle times, separate classroom spaces created, separate buses, and separate plans. Our children are often the objects of bullying, sometimes even by the adults entrusted with their care.

An autism label can take away the ability to look at these children as individuals. The darkness that settles in on a family, and the clawing desperation known only to parents of children who are misunderstood or called derogatory names by classmates, is the reason I began my quest. I decided if I could find even one "can" in my son, then it was possible to discover it in other children. And once I looked—very, very closely—I found that it was there.

People thought I was crazy to hope that there might be ability in my son and in the other children I worked with. Convinced that I was embracing false hope, they laughed at me and begged me to place him in more therapy. But I learned there is no such thing as false hope. There is only hope. And hope is a choice.

To be able to go through life from hour to hour and thrive while others consider you disabled would seem an unachievable goal. To decide each and every day that it is worth it to do your best—despite being told you can do nothing at all—is a true testimony to persistent hope. What strength and tenacity would it take to overcome everyone's doubts in your community? How could anyone get through being told "no" or "impossible" hundreds of times a day and still move forward? The courage it takes to break through autism is both hard to fathom and humbling. But one by one, in communities across the world, these children did just that. Their lives are the evidence—contradictory to science itself—that hope and faith can solve all things.

Today, young adults with autism are business owners, scientists, writers, speakers, theologians, and doctors. They are inventors, artists, musicians, and comedians. They make contributions to society and add beauty to our lives. Shining as a powerful light and testimony to others who are being told the very words they once heard, they are the reason not to despair, the evidence of ability lost in a previous generation.

One by one in city by city around the world, I have looked for people like Ron who are using what I call the "Spark" in their lives, and I am finding it! As these souls show us what they can do, we shatter perceptions, make the road easier for those who follow us, and enter a new awareness of autism.

Ron Sandison is a friend who walked a path many would describe as "outside the box." The choices he and his family had to make to put this book in your hands are extraordinary. They had to stop listening to practically everything and everyone who told them all day long, "Ron won't be able to…" By writing this book, he joins in a common mission with my son, Jacob, who published his first research paper in theoretical physics at age twelve; with Mikey Brannigan, one of the fastest high school mile runners in the United States; with Anthony Ianni, who played in the Final Four basketball tournament for Michigan State; and with comedian Michael McCreary, who, despite Asperger's, keeps his audiences rolling on the floor with laughter.

We can also see evidence of this "Spark" of ability in Clay Marzo, one of the world's top surfers; Alexis Wineman, who walked across a stage and became Miss Montana; Talina Toscano, who sang with a perfect pitch the songs she wrote at Carnegie Hall; Anthony Starego, who despite an IQ of only fifty-three, kicked two field goals to help his high school team win the state championship; and—from the previous generation—Dr. Temple Grandin, a professor with a PhD.

I am so glad I searched for these wonderful individuals. They are all capable adults who happen to have autism. And I am happy they are speaking out because they give us something new to look for: possibility.

Reading a new book has always been one of my favorite things to do. To read a book that seemed impossible to write just makes me smile. Despite every expert's predictions, Ron's natural talent and ability shine through these pages.

He is not living a disorder, nor is he a face that comes after a label. He is just Ron, an accomplished author who happens to have autism. My hope is the book you hold in your hands may help you enter your child's world, see his or her endless possibilities, and find hope no matter what others tell you. To find that hope requires silencing the skeptics who say "can't."

—Kristine Barnett
Author of the Best Seller
The Spark: A Mother's Story of Nurturing Genius

Chapter 1

UNDERSTANDING AUTISM

I KNEW THIS WOULD happen if I were the unlucky care specialist chosen to take the patient from our ward to the hospital on New Year's Day. Frustrated, my left hand began to shake. Reminding medical personnel to always clean their hands, the monitor in front of me at the nurse's station kept flashing: "Wash In; Wash Out." My brain already felt numb, unable to process any more information. I had spent the past eight hours sitting in a dimly lit room, reading my book on Christian publishing while I waited to see what would happen. Just then, a nurse gently opened the door and told me, "Dial 9 for an outside line, then the area code. We already have five inches of snow, so the roads will be slick!"

Pacing nervously along the linoleum floor, I contemplated, "It's already 4:00 p.m. My shift should have ended thirty minutes ago, and my reserve is still not here. I will be stuck here all night and miss the holiday." I reflected back to high school, twenty years earlier. Back then, I had to lift weights every day at 4:00 p.m.—just as Raymond, the lead character in *Rain Man,* had to watch *Jeopardy* at five o'clock!

This perfectionistic, obsessive behavior enabled me as a high school senior to bench-press over 260 pounds and run on the 3,200-meter relay track team; we set a new school record. Now, while the game had changed, the rules were similar. However, in place of metal weights, I utilized three-by-five-inch memory cards. My two- to three-hour memorization routine began right after work and had empowered me to quote more than ten thousand scriptures. This included twenty-two books of the New Testament and more than five thousand famous quotes from other sources. As the legendary British evangelist Charles Spurgeon once said, "By perseverance, the snail made it on the ark."[1]

Finally, impatient with the never-ending wait, I dialed the number of my own hospital. The receptionist didn't answer until the sixth ring: "Hello. How may I direct your call?"

"Put the charge nurse on the phone!" I blurted.

"Hold on for one moment," she replied.

As I waited, a soothing voice assured: "Our hospital is located on the scenic Lake Galloway in Oakland County and is an inpatient hospital with 251 beds—yada, yada, yada," before repeating endlessly. My irritation reached new heights. After what seemed like eons, a voice said, "Hello, Nurse Cindy."

"Where is my replacement staff? I have to get home now for my two hours of memory work!"

That's what bothered me most. Not that coming home late meant missing out on holiday time with our family. Or the bowl games. Or a relaxed dinner with my beautiful wife, Kristen. The delay would sabotage my daily memory routine and Bible studies. I follow this rigid schedule because of my autism. Yet, if you offered me a red pill that would cure me of my pattern-driven lifestyle, or swat me in the head with a magic mallet to smash my obsessive-compulsive behavior for Bible memorization, I would refuse. These patterns are the very gifts that make me who I am.

A BLESSED ROUTINE

In four decades of life I have never missed a day of work or even a single class in college, where class-cutting is endemic. My routine empowered me to graduate from Oral Roberts University

(ORU) with a master of divinity degree and a perfect 4.0 grade point average. My fixed study patterns equipped me to invest more than 35,000 hours in Bible memorization and studies, and led to my serving as an intern with the ministry of noted Bible teacher Jack Van Impe. If these tendencies and patterns were surgically extirpated from my life, I would lose the many blessings I have received from God—and the call to help those with learning disabilities and mental health issues.

At 5:00 p.m. my replacement finally arrived. Outside, I climbed into a waiting taxi-van. During the snowy drive back the driver shared with me his testimony of financial hardships and his faith in Christ, reflected by the cross dangling from his rearview mirror. As I exited the van, I handed the driver a tip. Our conversation reminded me that my memorization routine should never take precedence over people or my appreciation for all the spiritual and financial blessings God has given me. For a brief moment as I waved good-bye, this realization broke my cherished pattern.

If you were to meet me while in line at a Walmart, or hear me preach at your church, you would probably never guess that I have overcome a major learning disability. Were we to become acquainted, you would notice my autistic tendencies in subtle ways. For example, on my cell phone, Kristen is listed not as my wife but "Kristen from Bloomfield" (the city she lived in when we first met). Many individuals with Asperger's syndrome, one of the conditions on the autism spectrum, refer to themselves or others in the third person. A buddy from college used to joke, "Ron, when you are totally focused telling one of your stories, I could be standing in front of you on crutches having lost my leg to gangrene, and you would be so focused on sharing your ideas that you would never notice."

On 1/7/14 (the way I recall specific dates) Metro Detroit experienced a record low of minus fifteen degrees, with a windchill of minus forty degrees. I again demonstrated my odd behavior by arriving at work forty minutes early and doing thirty minutes of memory work in my shoebox-sized Saturn Ion—with the heat off. By the end of this exercise my fingers and toes felt frozen. As autism expert Dr. Michael D. Powers wrote in his book, *Asperger Syndrome & Your Child*, "Often times, adults with Asperger's Syndrome have adjusted so well and have so successfully modified their stand-out behaviors, that although they still have a lifelong disability, they do not appear disabled to casual observers."[2]

I have learned simple techniques for coping with autistic behavior, which I will share with you throughout this book. These methods will help educators, care workers, and families with children of autism. This concise guide shares real-life experiences, practical applications, and insights from my own life, as well as dozens of parents, professionals, educators, and volunteers sharing their experiences loving and serving children with autism—and the impact these children have had on them.[3]

Stigma of Autism

You knew it all along—ever since observing your seven-year-old son's early social interactions. Yet you were afraid to acknowledge his odd behavior and awkwardness in relationships with his peers. At birthday parties, while the other children played and rushed to watch the blowing out of the candles, your son, Mark, would sit isolated behind a chair, silently playing with his handheld Nintendo. Other parents would tell you, "Mark is just an introvert and will someday come out of his shell." Yet deep in your heart you knew he was different and would need special help.

Parents fear the crushing diagnosis of autism spectrum disorder (ASD) and also the stigma and labels attached with it. (See appendix A, where I list the advantages and disadvantages of labeling.) When their precious son or daughter is diagnosed with ASD, among the questions they ask themselves are: "What could we have done differently? Was there any prenatal care we could have taken to prevent this?" And the most painful: "God, why did it happen to our family?"

Every year in America between thirty-four thousand and sixty thousand families will receive a diagnosis that their son or daughter has ASD. More children will be diagnosed with autism this year than with AIDS, diabetes, and cancer—combined. This disorder is four to five times more prevalent in males than in females. Every eight minutes another child in the United States is diagnosed with autism. Overall, one in every six children will have a developmental disability. They range from mild disabilities, such as speech and language impairments, to serious developmental disabilities, such as intellectual disabilities (mental retardation), cerebral palsy, and autism.[4]

Early diagnosis of ASD can help prevent its debilitating effects. According to recent studies, such diagnosis and intervention can cut the lifetime cost of treatment by half. It is unknown if the dramatic rise in ASD statistics (as high as 600 percent since the 1980s) is due to better diagnostic tests or genetic, social, and environmental factors.[5] (See Simon Baron-Cohen's theory for this increased prevalence of autism in appendix A.)

The Autism Society estimates that the lifetime cost of caring for a child with ASD ranges from $3.5 million to $5 million. Annually the United States spends around $90 billion on autism, a figure that includes research, insurance costs and non-covered expenses, Medicaid waivers for autism, educational spending, housing, transportation, and employment, in addition to related therapeutic services and caregiver costs.[6]

Even with early detection, some of the stigmas of ASD will have a permanent impact on the child over his or her lifespan—people like Jim. In his mid-fifties, Jim had a PhD in philosophy from a prominent university, was a successful college professor, and taught classes on social change. Jim's Asperger's condition caused him to display such odd behavior as carrying a worn man-purse everywhere and having almost no eye contact with others during conversation. His family hired me to visit their elderly mother, Molly, three days a week. Molly suffered from dementia. When I entered the nursing home dayroom, Molly would beam as she exclaimed, "There's my favorite bridge partner!" (Ironically, I had never played this card game.)

Whenever her son Jim left after a visit, she would look at me and say, "My son Jim is brilliant, but he has a disorder that causes him to be peculiar and carry a worn-out purse." Because of her dementia, Molly couldn't remember the day of the week, the year, the president's name, or mine. Yet she never forgot that her beloved son was peculiar. Imagine your whole life your family and acquaintances referring to you as peculiar or strange. What causes ASD to have this effect? And what are some signs?

AUTISM SPECTRUM

The word *autism* is derived from the Greek word *autos*, which means self—as in autonomous. It has been used to describe individuals who appear to be self-contained or isolated in their own world, apart from general society.[7] A simple definition of autism is a physical condition linked to abnormal biology and chemistry in the brain. ASD is characterized by social deficits and communication difficulties, stereotyped or repetitive behaviors and interests, and—in some cases—cognitive delays.

The five main subgroups of autism are:

- Autistic disorder
- Asperger's syndrome
- Pervasive development disorder, or PDD-NOS

- Rett's syndrome
- Childhood disintegrative disorder, also known as Heller's syndrome and disintegrative psychosis (It is characterized by developmental delays in language, social functioning, and motor skills.)

Some children on the autism spectrum are severely affected in most or all domains of mental functioning, while others suffer only mildly. The National Research Council stated, "There is no single behavior that is always typical of autism and behavior that would automatically exclude an individual child from a diagnosis of autism."[8] Author Lynda Young, who encourages and advises families with children suffering from chronic health conditions, says, "If you've met one child on the spectrum, you've met one child on the spectrum. They're all different."[9]

In the revised *Diagnostic and Statistical Manual of Mental Disorder* (DSM-5, released in May of 2013), ASD is clinically diagnosed based on the symptoms and severities of traits in relationship to social communication symptoms, severity of fixated or restricted behaviors, or interests and associated features. Under DSM-V, there is only one ASD with three levels of severity. Based on these three, ASD can cause impaired social interaction; problems with verbal and nonverbal communication; and unusual, repetitive, or severely limited activities and interests. ASD specialist Lisa Jo Rudy observes:

> Autism is a spectrum disorder, meaning you can be a little autistic or very autistic. Until May, 2013, there were five official autism spectrum diagnoses, but the diagnoses within the ASD weren't clearly named, nor were the symptoms always the same even within the same diagnosis. What's worse, terms like severe autism, mild autism and high functioning autism are not true clinical

diagnoses—they are just descriptive terms to help parents
and educators understand a child's status on the ASD.[10]

When your son or daughter is diagnosed with ASD, specialists usually classify the functional level, ranging from mild
to severe. This level is determined by the individual's ability
to function and interact in society. Understanding how psychologists and other medical professionals assign these different levels can help you better understand this diagnosis.
The severe end includes individuals who are unable to function in society. At the other end are "peculiar" people, like Dr.
Jim (and me), who can lead independent, accomplished lives.

The Spectrum

Severe ASD

Severe ASD includes classic autism, childhood disintegrative disorder, or Rett's syndrome. Almost all children
diagnosed with severe ASD will never be able to function
independently and will require continual care throughout
their lives. Rett's syndrome is a rare genetic disorder that
primarily affects females. Some of the main traits of severe
autism include impaired mental or cognitive functioning, lack
of language skills, severe behavioral concerns, and an inability
to interact with their social environment.[11]

Twenty-five percent of all individuals with ASD are unable to
speak. Between 11 percent and 39 percent have a medical condition of seizure disorders or epilepsy. Approximately 50 percent
of individuals with autism are diagnosed with intellectual disability. Only about 10 percent of autistics belong in the "savant"—
or genius—category (though most savants are autistic).[12]

William Stillman, author of *The Soul of Autism*, shares one
mother's compassionate counsel for parents with children
unable to communicate verbally:

The point is to always presume intellect in your child. What this means is just because your child is nonverbal or severely autistic, don't assume that this means your child is not capable of understanding, thinking and feeling. A lot of parents, people in society, make the huge mistake of thinking that just because a child is autistic, and/or nonverbal, that they must be ignorant or stupid, or otherwise. They talk down to them and over them.

A child with a developmental delay may have deficits in many areas, but this does not mean that the child is unintelligent or unable to comprehend. Think of a deaf person, for example; do we consider him to be less intelligent because he is unable to hear? A person who has had a stroke may be unable to tell you what she wants, but she can understand what you say. If your child is not [impaired], then you should always presume intelligence and treat him/her accordingly.[13]

Moderate ASD

Moderate ASD can include classic autism, childhood disintegrative disorder, Rett's syndrome, or PDD-NOS. Individuals with moderate ASD traits usually require some assistance. Still, they may also have some degree of independence with their jobs and lives. There are characteristics of moderate ASD: normal or below normal mental functioning, difficulty communicating, mild behavioral concerns, or the appearance of aloofness.

High-functioning ASD

Mild or high-functioning ASD features include Asperger's syndrome, PDD-NOS, and classic high-functioning autism. Asperger's syndrome is often not diagnosed until a child reaches at least six years of age, and often later—including as late as adulthood.[14]

Tony Attwood, another expert on autism, says, "There is currently no convincing argument or data that unequivocally confirm that High Functioning Autism and Asperger's Syndrome are two separate and distinct disorders."[15]

Many people with Asperger's and mild ASD live and work independently. Characteristics can include normal or above-normal intelligence, normal skills (although with some communication challenges), minimal behavioral concerns, or socially atypical behavior. Five to 10 percent of children with autism possess strong memorization skills.

Other conditions that may accompany mild ASD are genetic disorders, intellectual or learning disabilities, anxiety disorder, and sleep deprivation.

Research indicates that around 65 percent of adolescents with Asperger's have an affective or mood disorder. The most common is an anxiety disorder. About 25 percent of adults with Asperger's also have clinical signs of obsessive-compulsive disorder, often known by its acronym, OCD.

A child with proper treatment and therapy can experience drastic improvement in his or her level of functioning. Parents should not focus solely on the ASD level but also on the child's growth and development. Melanie Fowler, whose son William was diagnosed with PDD-NOS, encourages parents, "If you're disheartened by a diagnosis or the seemingly limitless mountain you have before you to climb, keep in mind that a diagnosis or label is not a death sentence—children absolutely change as they grow, and some children may exhibit more typical and less autistic behavior as they get older."[16]

The goal of treatment should be to lessen association deficits and family stress from ASD, increase the quality of life for the child, and help him or her to be functionally independent.

RISK FACTORS

Research still cannot pinpoint the specific cause of ASD, only the risk factors. When a friend, family member, or student is diagnosed with ASD, you should be nonjudgmental and offer love and acceptance. Research has identified many risk factors, believed to be both genetically and environmentally related. They include genetics, prenatal and perinatal factors, environmental factors, and neuroanatomical abnormalities. Research studies from twins seem to demonstrate that genetics has a strong influence in the causes of autism and other pervasive developmental disorders. These studies indicate that the prevalence of autism in siblings of autistic children is approximately 15 to 30 percent greater than in the general population. Research also indicates that the parents' psychiatric history can contribute to ASD.[17]

Prenatal and perinatal factors include the age of the parents. Women over age forty are 77 percent more likely than women under twenty-five to bear a child with autism. Men over age forty are twice as likely as those in their mid- to late twenties to father a child with autism—but only if the mother is under age twenty-five.[18] As an example, my father, Chuck, was forty years old, while my mom, Janet, was twenty-four when I was born. Other prenatal- and perinatal-related risks are bleeding after the first trimester, use of certain prescription medications during pregnancy, meconium in the amniotic fluid, and gestational diabetes.

The term "environmental risk" refers to any influences other than changes by inherited genes that can cause a negative impact on the child's normal development. These risk factors for ASD include exposure to chemicals and pollutants, maternal nutrition, infections during pregnancy, and premature birth.

The final ASD risk factor involves neuroanatomical abnormalities. A recent study suggested that approximately 30 percent of persons with ASD have increased head size and brain volume. The largest study evaluating age-related changes in brain size in subjects from twelve months to fifty years of age showed early brain overgrowth during infancy and the toddler years in children with ASD, followed by an accelerated rate of decline in size and perhaps degeneration with age.[19] Longtime pediatrics specialist Dr. Margaret L. Bauman writes: "Based largely on the constellation of symptoms that characterize the disorder, various anatomical sites within the brain have been suggested as a possible primary source of pathology in autism."[20]

Based on his years of in-depth research, Yale psychologist Robert T. Schulz suggests that abnormalities in the amygdala may explain some of the symptoms of Asperger's syndrome in relationship to emotional impairment. Prefrontal cortex deficits in people with Asperger's appear to relate to their inability to experience empathy toward others.[21]

Early Warning Signs

Autism is normally first identified in children at age two; most children with ASD have significant symptoms by the time they reach their third birthday.[22] Some of the main warning signs for an infant include avoidance of eye contact, indifference to parents' touch, lack of apparent interest in others, or resistance to cuddling and holding. Normally a child smiles by age one and laughs when you play with him or her. If you point at the child's favorite teddy bear, he or she will look in that direction. Children also imitate sounds and facial expressions. A deficiency in these typical childhood behavior patterns could be an indicator of neurological problems.

Symptoms of ASD in children between one and three include[23]:

- Repetitive moments (flapping their hands, head-banging, rocking, spinning, or other self-stimulating behavior)

- Hypersensitivity to sounds, lights, or odors
- Fascination with parts of toys instead of the toy itself
- Tantrums when their daily pattern is altered or a transition is necessary
- Atypical communication patterns, including an inability to speak, temporary loss of language previously learned, or a delay in language acquisitions
- Failing to engage in make-believe activities with their peers and appearing to remain isolated or aloof from others

While there is no cure for autism, therapy and treatment can help provide the environment and skills for your child to reach his or her maximum potential, as well as limit autism's debilitating effects. Early diagnosis is critical and will help your child quickly receive the intervention required for language development, behavior management, social interaction, and learning skills.

WHAT NOW?

If your son Mark (I will use this name throughout the book for illustrative purposes) has been diagnosed with ASD, what should you do? Here are ten quick points that can help you and your family to deal with this diagnosis.

First, realize that while this diagnosis may feel crushing now and change your expectations for your child's life, it is not the end of the world. Many people—like Dr. Jim, author Temple Grandin, professor Stephen Mark Shore, and me— have been able to overcome the debilitating effects of autism and live meaningful, successful lives.

Second, discover your child's personal strengths and weaknesses. Mark may have some undiscovered gift or unique talent, such as memorization, music, chess, or computer skills, which will empower him to overcome his deficits. I love these two proverbs from King Solomon: "A gift opens the way for the giver and ushers him into the presence of the great" (Prov. 18:16), and "Do you see a man skilled in his work? He will serve before kings; he will not serve before obscure men" (Prov. 22:29). As Dr. Shore says, "Realize your child has great potential and help him or her to reach it."[24]

Third, recognize your son or daughter's weaknesses so you can provide an environment in which he or she will be able to flourish and mature. Many children with ASD have a hypersensitivity to certain sounds, lights, odors, touch, or tastes. (I will examine sensory issues in the next chapter.) When I am studying or doing memory work, the sound of a vacuum or loud music causes me to feel severe anxiety and lose my ability to concentrate; as a child, I would scream and cover my ears when a noise disturbed me. Other children with ASD find soft music enhances their ability to focus and makes them feel calm and safe.

Fourth, discover the learning style that works best for your child and will enable him or her to comprehend and apply information. Individuals can be visual, verbal, logical, aural, or physical learners, or a combination of these. Computers also can provide a powerful educational tool. Educational pioneer John Dewey once noted that understanding arises from activity, like the kind computers can provide.

Many children with autism and learning disabilities have more than one disability that can hinder their education and development. In my elementary and high school years I had great difficulty learning phonetically because of an auditory processing disorder (APD). My freshman year of high school, I received a D in Spanish because I was unable to learn a foreign language through phonetic repetition. (Three different times the teacher sent me to detention for behavior problems.)

Ten years later, when this same teacher saw my mom at a supermarket and heard I had become a preacher, she reacted with amazement, commenting, "Ron, unlike his older brother, Steve, was always a troublemaker in my class and flunked every test." Yet, during my master's degree studies at Oral Roberts University, I took biblical Greek for three years and had a perfect 4.0 grade point average. I learned the language not by phonetics but visually with vocabulary and grammatical flashcards—which enabled me to use my gift of memorization.

Fifth, research every resource available—books, therapy journals, organizations, and available treatments. Use all of this to help your child reach his or her full potential. As Solomon wrote, "If the ax is dull and its edge unsharpened, more strength is needed, but skill will bring success" (Eccles. 10:10). These resources and programs can help your son or daughter learn the skills needed for an independent and successful life.

Sixth, be an advocate for your child to receive accommodation to help him or her in school. Insist teachers allow unlimited time for taking tests and special tutoring for subjects he or she finds difficult.

Seventh, teach your child to be his or her own advocate and to possess the confidence to ask for help when he or she needs it. Promote self-advocacy through self-knowledge and self-awareness. If your child is low-functioning or mentally impaired and unable to be his or her own advocate, teach other siblings (or, if none are available, a friend) to act as advocates.

Eighth, help your child obtain mentoring from school peers. My coworker Toby Evans—who served six years in public schools as a care-worker for autistic students—said, "The best opportunities and teaching an autistic child can receive is a program like Link, a mentoring program that allows children in special education classes to interact with regular education students and thus develop relationship and life skills. Some of the students in our Link program developed life-time friend-ships."[25] Or, as Proverbs puts it, "As iron sharpens iron, so one person sharpens another" (Prov. 27:17).

Ninth, develop creative techniques to alter your child's fixed routines or exclusive interests. Most children with autism follow rigid patterns and fixed routines, which causes change of any kind to be quite challenging. In my case, moving from Rochester Hills, Michigan, to Tulsa, Oklahoma, for college posed an immense challenge. I adjusted for this transition by studying the Tulsa area and recognizing the rewards of obtaining a degree from a respected Christian institution. My parents also encouraged me to go "by faith."

If your family is moving to a different state due to a spouse's job, you can help smooth the transition for your child by having him or her explore the city online, or through books, and discover benefits of the new location. If your child loves dinosaurs, have him or her check the pictures of the museum of science. This offers children a sense of control and will make them feel an important part of the family's decision.

If your child has an obsessive focus on a certain interest or topic, you can help him or her to become less rigid by offering alternative activities. In the aforementioned *Asperger Syndrome & Your Child*, Dr. Powers shares the testimony of parents with an autistic child, Ethan, who obsessed over the train schedule. Ethan would obsessively check and recheck the schedule to see if the Metro North train would be early or delayed. His parents helped tame this dragon of orderliness by only allowing him to check the schedule twice a day at prearranged times.[26]

As a child, I grew obsessive about prairie dogs and carried a ten-and-a-half-inch stuffed animal, Prairie Pup, to school until I reached sixth grade. My parents creatively broke this age-inappropriate pattern by prohibiting Prairie Pup from attending public school. Instead of relying on my stuffed friend, they encouraged me to get involved in track and football.

Finally, remain flexible. Children with ASD can cause parents (and possibly siblings) to feel emotionally and spiritually drained. Accept your child's limitations, and learn to adjust your life to the challenges ahead. Also, pray for grace. Remember the message Paul wrote to the Corinthians, which is quite appropriate here: "And God is able to make all grace abound in you, so that in all things at all times, having all that you need, you will abound in every good work" (2 Cor. 9:8). God will provide you with the power to endure, so cling to these words from Paul's letter to the Colossians: "To this end I strenuously contend with all the energy Christ so powerfully works in me" (Col. 1:29).

Summary

There is no cure for autism, but with love and acceptance, we can help children with ASD reach their full potential and bring glory to God. Because ASD exists along a spectrum, we should never stereotype children with ASD. Some children with ASD are high-functioning and experience only mild difficulty in social settings, while others are nonverbal and have extreme difficulty interacting with others.

Now that you have a basic overview of ASD, let's explore insiders' perspectives and the impact this condition can have on your child and family.

Chapter 2

INSIDERS' PERSPECTIVES

A s mentioned in chapter 1, the varying degrees along the autism spectrum void the idea of a one-size-fits-all diagnosis. In this chapter I will examine insiders' perspectives of ASD's features and methods to help limit its debilitating effects. Among the unique traits I will explore are lack of empathy (or mind-blindness), echolalia (use of repetitive phrases), the inability to interpret social clues (awkwardness), repetitive behavior, tantrums, literal interpretation, acute sensory sensitivities, stimming (self-stimulatory behavior), dysgraphia (difficulty with handwriting), and eccentric interests. Depending on the severity of the autism, your ASD child may have only a few of these traits, or many.

LACK OF EMPATHY

"Raise your hand if you know what empathy is," Stacy, a third-grade teacher, told her class. In response, little Teddy raised his hand high and said, "I don't know, and I don't care." Teddy's reaction demonstrates his failure to comprehend the meaning of empathy—the ability to understand and share another's feelings. Does every child with ASD lack this essential ingredient, or merely express concerns and compassion differently?

I compare this tendency to a shopping trip my wife, Kristen, and I made to PetSmart. As we walked the aisles looking for rabbit pellets for our bunny, Babs, we saw blue and white parakeets. I said to Kristen, "Maybe we should get Pre a new friend!" When I mentioned my idea to the sales associate, she asked, "Does your parakeet have a mirror?"

"Yes, Pre has a mirror," I replied. "She loves to sing and chirp at it day and night."

"Pre will never be able to accept a friend," the sales associate warned. "Mirrors cause birds to become self-absorbed and unable to interact with their environment."

This comment prompted me to go online, where I found a blog by bird lover Karen Trinkaus:

> The real problem is this: mirrors give your bird an incorrect perception of reality. They are NOT talking to another bird, they are talking to a reflection. Reflections can only mimic—they do not react in the same manner as a real bird would. Think of it this way: you have a young child. This is your only child so instead of letting him play with kids down the street you get him a mirror. The kid spends all his time talking and playing with his reflection. When he turns fifteen years old you send him to high school. How well do you think he's going to socialize with real people who may not agree with him, may not like his looks, may look different than him, etc.?[1]

Like Pre, some children with ASD are self-absorbed and experience great difficulty expressing feelings of empathy. Their habit of repeating certain phrases from their favorite movies or TV shows can increase this social awkwardness. In *Rain Main*, Raymond's echolalia that drove his younger brother, Charlie, nuts came from the legendary Abbott and Costello comedy sketch, "Who's on First?" To soothe his nerves, Raymond would repeat this phrase to overcome anxiety.

I once cared for Ben, a young adult with ASD. When nervous, he would repeat, "Dr. Luke, hey Ben. How are you doing,

Ben? Very good! Thank you, doctor." Ben's mother told me, "Dr. Luke is Ben's dentist, and my son loves to see his dentist because he wears bright orange, stylish shirts. Ben releases his stress by repeating this phrase and thinking of his favorite dentist." When Ben experienced anxiety and paced the floors, I would say, "Dr. Luke." Ben would quickly repeat his echolalia phrase, calmly sit down, and rock back and forth, smiling and giggling.

SELF-ABSORBED

The lack of emotion displayed by some self-absorbed children with ASD does not necessarily mean they lack concern or compassion; they just may express it differently. Instead of showing deep emotion, they may demonstrate empathy with loving actions. One of the tests for empathy in young children is to monitor their response to someone else receiving a shot in the arm. A typical child will cringe as he sees the needle enter another person's arm, especially if he or she has experienced pain from a needle prick. A typical ASD child, oblivious to the other person's pain, will display little or no response. Dr. Simon Baron-Cohen, director of the Autism Research Center at the University of Cambridge, refers to them as Zero-Positive because they lack empathy, but their high moral standards (patterns and behavior) cause them not to wish pain or evil on others. In his book *The Science of Evil* the professor of developmental psychopathology writes:

> Having empathy difficulties may be socially disabling, but empathy is not the sole route to developing a moral code and a moral conscience that leads a person to behave ethically. This is where we meet people who have zero degrees of empathy but who are Zero-Positive....Zero-Positive means that alongside difficulties with empathy, these individuals have remarkably precise, exact minds. They have

Asperger's Syndrome, a condition on the ASD. People with Asperger's Syndrome are Zero-Positive for two reasons.

First, in their case their empathy difficulties are associated with having a brain that processes information in ways that can lead to talent. Second, the way their brain processes information paradoxically leads to super-moral rather than immoral.[2]

Zero-Positive individuals have mind-blindness. They lack the social ability and the insight to see the world from another person's perspective, resulting in a lack of empathy. A few years ago a coworker—whose husband had recently died of cancer and was employed at our company for more than sixteen years—was fired. Because of a health condition, she was unable to perform required tasks due to her lack of mobility. When our supervisor took her keys and walked her out, I felt angry that our employer would not provide this faithful coworker with an office position. Instead of emotions, I displayed my empathy with actions of love. I wrote her a letter describing our clients' and staff's love for her and included a check.

My response of love compensated for my lack of inner feelings of empathy. As a child, my parents taught me to care for the needs of others, and not just with words, but with actions and truth. (See 1 John 3:18.) The Holy Spirit also brought to mind Psalm 68:5, which says God is "a father to the fatherless, a defender of widows." The Spirit's conviction, coupled with my parents' godly teaching, compelled me to take action.

If your child lacks empathy, teach him or her—in a concrete manner—to care for the needs of others with positive reinforcements (rewards) and by modeling love for those in need. As Paul said, "Follow my example, as I follow the example of Christ" (1 Cor. 11:1). With positive reinforcements, biblical teachings, and personal examples of concern, children with ASD will develop a pattern of empathy.

Mind-Blindness

Mind-blindness also causes difficulty with decoding social cues, interpreting people's facial expressions and body language, and understanding their inner thoughts and feelings. Dr. Albert Mehrabian, author of *Silent Messages*, estimates that more than 90 percent of communication is nonverbal. According to his research, only 7 percent of any message is conveyed through words, 38 percent through certain vocal elements, and 55 percent through nonverbal elements (such as facial expressions, gestures, or posture).[3] As you can see, this represents a major communication deficiency for an ASD child. Counselor Dr. Laura Henderson, whose son Eric has ASD, says:

> Because spectrum kids didn't pick up nonverbal communication, they're less able to make an educated guess about how someone else is feeling and what he may want. This makes them less able to understand the other person's point of view. Spectrum people are also less likely to be able to form an empathetic connection to the other person, that is, to "feel with" him. This also may be related to their difficulty grasping the cues others get from faces, tone of voice, and gestures.[4]

Facial expression flashcards (available online at the Autism Community Store[5]) are one method of helping your child interpret the meanings of facial expressions. These pictures will help your child to recognize different facial expressions and how to respond to them with empathy. You can also help your child decode social cues by teaching him or her to ask informative, direct questions like:

- "What are you thinking?"
- "Can you please explain what you mean by that statement?"

- "How does that make you feel?"

When my wife, Kristen, and I moved into our first apartment as newlyweds, we had everything we needed, except a couch. My procrastination in purchasing one upset her so much that she nudged me away when I tried to cuddle with her. Sensing her anger, I asked, "What are you thinking?"

"We need to get a couch before our Super Bowl party next week!"

My question enabled Kristen to share her feelings, which I sometimes have difficulty decoding. In the same way, Dr. Michael Powers recommends that if a son or daughter has difficulty understanding social situations, parents should teach him or her to model other children's actions on the playground. This helps reinforce their behavior with their peers and enables them to assimilate within the dynamics of their group.

Such learning is vital; Powers says the best hope children with ASD have of learning social situations is to develop their own critical thinking skills.[6] These skills will enable your child to understand cultural norms of behavior in various social settings. For example, it is socially acceptable to play on the jungle gym outside at the playground but not on a display inside Home Depot. A good curriculum for helping children's social skills is Carol Gray's *The New Social Story Book*, which instructs children with ASD through pictorially scripted scenarios in a concrete, sequential, and repetitive format.[7]

Another practical curriculum is the Picture Exchange Communication System (PECS). This system is designed for nonverbal children but can also help verbal children strengthen their communication skills. PECS uses six phases to teach children methods to ask questions, make comments, and express their desires. (For more information, see appendix A.) Melanie Fowler suggested making your own PECS flashcards:

You can find free black-and-white PECS pictures online. Cut them out, laminate them, buy some Velcro and a notebook binder, and you've got yourself a mobile pictorial system to take with you anywhere. Even if your child has words, extra visual cues help in explaining a situation and likely ease the anxiety and stress your child may be experiencing.

Explaining a trip to the doctor, dentist, or even grandma's house by using pictures to help them see and understand what is going to happen next can make a huge difference in the ease of daily activities, for both your child and you. When you see your child come unglued because of a slight transition, delay, or change of schedule, a PECS system created for and modeled after your own schedule use can be very helpful.[8]

TASMANIAN DEVIL

No matter how strong your faith in God, repetitive routines will challenge it. I recall the Facebook post I read from Kim, a Christian high school teacher whose son has autism. She talked of how her son had to have every Christmas gift in a particular spot under the tree or he would throw a tantrum. She noted that made her feel like sending him and his toys back to Santa Claus. Lynn Hamilton, the author of *Facing Autism*, says, "Many children throw tantrums when they don't get their way or a routine is broken. But a child with autism may have more extreme or longer-lasting tantrums."[9]

Every parent knows similar feelings. Mine certainly did. In recent years I observed another example of the need for routine while working with an eighteen-year-old whom I'll call Stan. His autism limited his communication ability to about ten words. His parents brought him to the hospital for medication adjustments and to avoid posing any danger to others. During his stay Stan would watch cartoons and rock back and forth in the chair farthest from the day lounge door. If any of the patients or staff attempted to change the station or sit in his chair, Stan would bite and scratch them. During commercials he paced the halls and flapped his hands in an up-and-down motion.

For the month I provided care for Stan, I had him follow the same repetitive schedule. He would eat breakfast, take his meds, pace the halls, and watch *Power Rangers*, *Scooby Doo*, and the *Flintstones*. This identical pattern helped him remain calm. When our supervisor assigned a coworker to watch Stan on an afternoon shift, I told him, "Make sure you follow the pattern—allow him to sit in his favorite seat, watch his cartoons, and if he touches your head, don't remove his hand."

The next day, when Robert arrived for the afternoon shift, he muttered, "Stan mutated into a Tasmanian devil yesterday. It happened in an instant. One of the patients was sitting in his chair, so I redirected him to another seat. As I was redirecting him, a patient changed the station from *Power Rangers* to *Charmed*, and Stan began biting my arm, screaming, and throwing a chair."

If you are the parent of a child who follows a rigid pattern, make sure to keep to his or her routine and use coping methods to help your child stay calm. For Stan, the flapping motion of his hands, sitting in his chair, touching the top of a head, and watching Cartoon Network helped release stress. Any change to this fixed schedule created great anxiety and fear, leading to the Tasmanian moment.

WORLD WAR III

It isn't just children and young adults who experience outbursts. For our first wedding anniversary, Kristen and I took a two-week vacation to Israel with her parents. Because of my ongoing chatter about the Bible history I had memorized, the travel guide for our group nicknamed me "The Preacher." At major biblical sites he would describe their historical and political significance and then ask me to share my insights with our fourteen-member group.

Our final week included a four-day stay at the David Citadel Hotel in Jerusalem. As we traveled from Tel Aviv to Jerusalem, our bus made a sightseeing stop at the historical City of David. There, I shared about the key events of King David's life and reign. Finally, around 7:30 p.m., our tired group arrived at the David Citadel Hotel. The wait staff greeted us with a selection of fresh orange and grapefruit juices, tasty dates, and dried apricots. As the bellboys hurried to shuttle our suitcases to our rooms, the hotel manager said, "We need to have your credit card information." No other hotel had asked for this information; the tour price included accommodations.

Exhibiting my autistic tendencies, my hand flew up in a half-V motion. Lunging at the surprised manager like a honey badger springing from his burrow, I shouted, "I have never had a credit card in my whole life because when you pay with plastic the amygdala section of your brain does not register loss aversion as it does with cash, causing you to spend more money! When you pay with cash, you experience an actual loss due to the amount of cash decreasing and your wallet becoming lighter. Also with OCD, a credit card could be disastrous and cause a tidal-wave of uncontrolled spending. Under international law your hotel has to accept cash the same as credit. Otherwise, nations could lose their sovereign power, due to no longer having the control of the currency!"

Like Dr. Spock, the famed *Star-Trek* character, my decisions were based on pure logic and empirical argument.

The wise manager replied politely, "Sorry, sir. Don't worry about a thing."

Though they never said anything, I'm sure my reaction

embarrassed my wife and in-laws. This reaction reflected a tantrum I had four years earlier while Kristen and I were dating. We often visited a theater multiplex on Thursday evenings because of the 50 percent discount. When I asked for two tickets to the movie we wanted to see, the high school-age clerk said, "Twenty dollars, please!"

Expecting to pay half that amount, I asked, "Did you discontinue the discount deal?"

"No, today is Veterans Day," the clerk said with a smile. "So it's holiday rate!"

Enraged, I demanded to speak with the manager—who echoed: "Our company policy is every holiday we charge regular price."

"I can prove to you that you don't consider Veterans Day a holiday!" I shouted. Turning to the clerk, I asked, "Do you receive time-and-a-half holiday pay for Christmas and the Fourth of July?"

"Yes."

"Are you getting holiday pay today?" I asked. When the clerk said, "No," I looked the manager in the eye and said, "If Veterans Day is considered by executives to be a holiday, why are your employees not receiving holiday pay?"

As the manager stood mute, I looked around the crowded lobby and asked, "How many veterans are here?" After two people responded, I said, "Thanks so much for risking your lives for our country and protecting our freedom. I just wanted to let you guys know that AMC is charging you double price today to show its patriotism!"

Not only did that make them angry, but also the manager gave us free gift cards for popcorn and drinks. Most people would have just accepted the fact that the theater was charging holiday rate on a Thursday. Not someone with autism and Asperger's. Things must stay the same—period.

Meltdowns

Many children with ASD also experience meltdowns. While related to tantrums, they represent a complete loss of control caused by overstimulation or health problems. In *Rain Man*, Raymond experienced a meltdown when frightened by the deafening noise of a fire alarm. Unable to move, he covered his ears, curled into a ball, and screamed. Special education examiner Robin Hansen explains the difference between a tantrum and a meltdown:

> Unlike tantrums, meltdowns can leave even experienced parents at their wit's end, unsure of what to do. When you think of a tantrum, the classic image of a child lying on the floor with kicking feet, swinging arms and a lot of screaming is probably what comes to mind. This is not even close to a meltdown. A meltdown is best defined by saying it is a total loss of behavioral control. It is loud, risky at times, frustrating, and exhausting.[10]

Given this prospect, learn to recognize warning signals of a pending tantrum or meltdown. Be alert and monitor these responses: pacing, hyperactivity, increased anxiety or agitation, hand-to-face repetitive motions, rocking back and forth, jumping side to side, intensified internal stimuli (talking to self), or excessive stimming (self-stimulatory behavior that helps soothe the child.) Says one of my coworkers, "Children with ASD have different warning signals. Fourteen-year-old John would repetitively tap his palm to his nose right before a major tantrum. I would gently redirect John to the water faucet, and the sound of running water would defuse his anxiety. Learning the child's unique coping mechanisms is essential. Repetitive motions and behavior can decrease anxiety but only temporarily."

In addition to learning their warning signs, seek to better

understand your child's coping mechanisms. If possible, teach him or her to use them to defuse anxiety and fear. Coping mechanisms can be as simple as running water, taking five deep breaths, reading a Bible memory verse, looking at pictures, or listening to soft, soothing music. My parents trained me from a young age to choose my battles wisely. Mom would say, "Ron, don't be like Don Quixote and tilt [fight] every windmill as if it were a real dragon." As Solomon instructed parents, "Train up a child in the way he should go, and when he is old he will not depart from it" (Prov. 22:6, MEV). The key to teaching is consistency.

LITERAL INTERPRETATION

I have already mentioned the difficulties ASD children have decoding social clues. Many struggle to interpret abstract concepts or accept figurative phrases literally. Autism advocate Gary Porter notes:

> A common characteristic of those on the autism spectrum is the difficulty in grasping abstract concepts, meaning non-tangible ideas, objects or things are often difficult to understand. Thus, the majority of those with autism are concrete thinkers and tend to focus on the 'here and now' and have difficulty in generalizations. Included in the concrete thought process is the propensity to take words or phrases literally. With the English language full of slangs, puns and paradoxes, this can pose a daunting challenge for the autistic mind.[11]

My sophomore year of high school, a food fight erupted in the cafeteria. Soon hamburgers and grilled cheese sandwiches decorated the floor. At 2:30 p.m. that afternoon the principal announced over the PA system: "Due to the food fight today, this coming Monday at lunchtime, all students must remain silently in their seats the whole hour, and no students are permitted to leave their chairs without permission."

Monday at lunch, I followed this order to the letter of the law as I sat down silently next to my best friend, Nate. Three pretty girls smiled at me and pointed to a vacant chair next to them. Meanwhile, the principal and faculty walked around the cafeteria, aggressively monitoring the situation. Smiling at the girls and winking, I picked up my seat with my back leaning forward so that I would continue to remain "seated" as I walked toward them.

His face quickly flushing crimson, the principal quickly approached with a staff member to each side. "Did you not hear the announcements today and Friday?" he asked. I smiled and politely replied, "Of course I did. That's why I made sure to remain in my seat. I did just as you instructed. As you can see, I remained in my chair the whole time!"

A humorous book with comical illustrations that creatively helps demonstrate the concrete thinking style of a child with ASD is *Unintentional Humor: Celebrating the Literal Mind* by Brent Anderson and Linda Gund Anderson. This book can help you teach your son or daughter—through visual representations and repetition—if they have difficulty interpreting abstract concepts or figurative phrases. For example, if your son does not comprehend the meaning of "surfing the web" and literally pictures himself on a surfboard, use a computer to give a visual demonstration of this phrase.

A supervisor and architect at General Motors, my father had little patience explaining instructions to a ten-year-old child on the method for mowing our one-acre yard. When I failed to cut the lawn the exact length or put the grass clippings in the designated spot—behind the house in the woods— he would get frustrated and lecture me. As a child with autism, I had great difficulty understanding instructions. To this day, I fear getting lost if I fail to precisely follow directions. Like me, if your child has difficulty with instructions, you can help by writing out directions with an explanation in easy-to-follow steps. Step one: put two gallons of gas mixed with one can of oil in the mower. Step two: press the pump button three times. Step three: pull the string to start the blade. It also helps to show by example and visual support.

"Teachers who truly want to help students with sensory and perception difficulties will figure out the child's unique learning style and adapt teaching methods accordingly," says author and ASD overcomer Temple Grandin. "Some children do best with written instructions and assignments; others will do best through oral methods or oral testing. The best teachers have a flexible approach and teach to the style through which each child learns."[12]

SENSORY OVERLOAD

The majority of people pay little attention to their senses. When we feel cold, we put on a sweater. When music is too loud, we turn down the volume. Yet, for some ASD children, senses can provide unreliable information, causing great discomfort and anxiety. They may experience sensory overload with touch, sound, taste, smell, or sight. Says Dr. Michael Powers:

> Children with ASD may experience hyposensitivity, or reduced or lessened sensitivity, in some situations, and seek unusual amounts of stimulation. It may be that some of the self-stimulation characteristic of children with ASD—fidgeting, rocking, or spinning of oneself or objects—is related to a need for more sensory input.[13]

"Sensory sensitivities are the uncomfortable, painful, or upsetting sensation you receive in reaction to sensory stimuli that are beyond your tolerance threshold," says prolific author

William Stillman. "These sensations relate to your five senses either singularly or in combination. For example, perhaps the scent of a certain food odor or strong perfume makes you feel nauseated or headachy, or you may have an aversion to both the sight and sound of a large crowd."[14] Following are some of the senses that can disturb ASD children.

Touch

An acute sense of touch may cause your child to wear only certain fabrics that feel comfortable and to dislike wool or other clothing materials. Your child may experience great discomfort with buttons and thus prefer T-shirts, or desire corduroy's soft texture over jeans. If your child has touch-sensitive issues, be alert to any clothing that may cause pain or create conflict. These include tight shoes, wool socks, and scratchy tags. Your child may also be acutely sensitive to temperature or the sensation of certain brands of shampoo on the head.

Sound

Many children with ASD have hypersensitive hearing. They experience pain from high-pitched or ringing sounds, such as vacuum cleaners, sirens, hair dryers, or fire alarms. In college I struggled with the noise of bass in my dormitory. Such sounds deafened my ears and felt like a thunderstorm. Grandin had similar experiences as a child: "When I was little, loud noises were also a problem, often feeling like a dentist's drill hitting a nerve. They actually caused pain. I was scared to death of balloons popping, because the sound was like an explosion in my ear. Minor noises that most people can tune out drove me to distraction.[15]

There are three types of sounds that can be perceived as extremely unpleasant.

1. Sudden, unexpected noises

2. High-pitched, continuous sounds

3. Confusing, complex, or multiple sounds[16]

Taste

Your child may have an acute sensory response to the taste or texture of certain foods, which affects his or her eating habits. Melanie Fowler's son, William, is a picky eater. So she and her husband, Seth, established a household rule that their children must take a small bite of everything they serve. This rule helped William to be receptive to trying new foods and not just feast on chicken nuggets and french fries. Special foods or drinks can also be used as reinforcement for positive behavior. The young man, Ben, I mentioned previously, loves Diet Coke. So the staff would give him a cup, but only if he followed his treatment plan for that shift.

Smell

Some children have such an acute sensory response to smell. Odors that are undetectable to most people may cause them a severe migraine headache or nausea. The odors of bleach, paint, and varnish cause me to experience migraines; I can smell them a week after their application. If your child has an acute reaction to certain odors, make sure when you use those items to keep windows open to allow breezes to air out your house.

Sight

Lighting may also have a negative impact on your son or daughter and affect your child's ability to learn in the classroom. They may feel disoriented or discomforted by bright or flashing lights. If children hold objects close to their eyes, roll their head from side to side, prefer dark areas, try to continually pick up tiny pieces of paper or dust particles, stare at objects or shiny things, or look at people with a blank stare, they may be dealing with a visual sensory concern.

In such cases, it is important to prevent sensory overload, which can result in negative behavior, fear, anxiety, withdrawal, increased repetitive behavior, tantrums, or a complete meltdown. Understanding your child's range of arousal can help prevent overstimulation. As Lynn Hamilton says: "A child's ability to learn depends greatly on his level of stimulation. If a child has hyposensitivities, his body may be understimulated, making him inattentive to his surroundings. On the other hand, if a child's senses get overstimulated, he may become overactive, or he may go to the other extreme and actually 'shutdown' to protect himself."[17]

Grandin also warns parents and teachers to be aware of the signs of sensory problems:

> Watch your child closely—the signs are there. Do you see him putting his hands over his ears to block out noise? Does he become agitated every time you're in a bustling, noisy, or chaotic environment? Are there certain textures of food he just will not tolerate? Do you find her pulling at or taking off clothes that have rough textures or tugging at necklines where tags are rubbing?
>
> Children and adults who have tantrums and cannot tolerate being in a large supermarket, such as Wal-Mart, are almost certain to have sensory problems. Also note: tolerance levels quickly diminish when the individual is tired or hungry. For example, a child may tolerate a large grocery store in the morning but not during the afternoon.[18]

Teach your child appropriate coping methods for self-regulating overstimulation situations through such means as meditation, listening to calm music, taking deep breaths, or by showing him or her Scripture cards or pictures. These techniques can enable your child to monitor the level of sensory input and remain calm.

STIMMING

One of the common attributes associated with ASD is stimming (self-stimulating behavior), also referred to as stereotypical behavior. For individuals with ASD, stimming behavior helps them manage stress, fear, anxiety, and overwhelming sensory input. When you bite your nails, tap your pencil, twirl your hair, or pace around in a circle, you are engaging in this pattern. Animals release stress this way too. My rabbit, Babs, thumps her hind leg when she is excited or nervous. When I experience anxiety, I sometimes tap my index and middle fingers continually on the side of my head.

Children with ASD may display such behavior as flapping their hands up and down, pacing in circles, rocking back and forth, jumping from side to side, or spinning their whole body. As blogger Lisa Ro Rudy says: "Unlike most people, though, individuals with autism may self-stimulate constantly, and stimming may stand between them and their ability to interact with others, take part in ordinary activities, or even be included in typical classrooms. A child who regularly needs to pace the floor or slap himself in the head is certain to be a distraction for typical students."[19]

If your child's stimming is a hindrance to educational development and interaction with peers, applied behavior analysis therapy (ABA) can help eliminate or modify it. (I will examine this form of therapy in greater detail in chapter 8.) Dr. Lynn Kern Koegel, cofounder of the Autism Research Center at the University of California at Santa Barbara, recommends such therapy to limit stimming:

Many children with autism learn to redirect their urges to stim into more appropriate activities, often ones that have the same type of sensory input that the original stim supplied. It may not be considered socially acceptable to wiggle threads or flap your hands in public; it is socially acceptable to knit, draw at a table, or play a piano for hours on end.

You can help lead your child toward appropriate behaviors, which may in time even become strengths. We know many children with autism who once had high levels of stim and who are now award-winning runners, accomplished artists, and successful musicians.[20]

Dysgraphia

Many children with ASD have dysgraphia, which is the inability to write coherently. Often they struggle with the mechanics of writing. I spoke my first word, "mama," at nine months of age. Like many children with ASD, eighteen months later I began to regress and lose my language ability.

Tutoring and therapy enabled me to overcome learning disabilities. My parents saved money for my brothers' and my education. As a result, in childhood I had tutors to help me learn to read and write. My parents invested their own time helping me develop my writing skills and with homework. If I ever needed help with a project or studying for a test, they were always there for me. In the next chapter on parenting I will discuss in detail the challenges of helping your child overcome his or her disabilities.

Eccentric Interest

Some ASD children have an eccentric interest in airplanes, trains, automobiles, computers, music, animals, sports statistics, or other narrow topics. As mentioned in the first chapter,

I carried a stuffed Prairie Pup everywhere until I reached the sixth grade. My fourth-grade teacher told my mom, "Ron always has in one arm Prairie, and in the other a book on animals." My obsession caused me to be an expert on animals—especially prairie dogs. I still collect the toy animals Calico Critters and Sylvanian Families. Our wedding cake even had Calico Critters bride-and-groom cats and a beaver priest.

As a parent, not only encourage your child to learn information on a particular passion, but also help him or her to broaden the topics they study. One method is teaching your child how other subjects relate to a favorite interest. If your child loves trains but hates algebra, set up a fifteen-minute break from algebra study to enjoy playtime with trains.

Summary

As you have seen, the autism spectrum varies greatly and has many unique characteristics. Through therapy, coping mechanisms, and care, your ASD child can overcome many debilitating effects and live a meaningful life. As a parent, don't allow labels to dictate your perspectives; encourage your children to reach their full potential. As Grandin encourages, "The best thing a parent of a newly diagnosed child can do is to watch one's child, without preconceived notions and judgments and learn how the child functions, acts, and reacts to his or her world."[21]

Even with the best therapy and education, autism features will manifest themselves. As I wrote this book, I used laser-sharp concentration until I finished. When I became anxious trying to determine the precise word I wanted to use, my self-regulating stimming technique began, causing me to tap the side of my head with my index and middle fingers. *New York Times* best-selling author John Elder Robison wrote of his Asperger's:

As I recall my own development, I can see how I went through periods where my ability to focus inward and do complex calculations in my mind developed rapidly. When that happened, my ability to solve complex technical or mathematical problems increased, but I withdrew from other people. Later, there were periods where my ability to turn toward other people and the world increased by leaps and bounds. At those times, my intense powers of focused reasoning seemed to diminish.[22]

Encourage your child to interact with peers and avoid withdrawing or becoming self-absorbed. Through interaction your child can develop social skills and experience emotions. Join support groups for children with ASD, and get involved in your child's treatment plan. Above all, never lose hope. As Susan, the mother of an autistic son, says:

No matter what diagnosis our children are given, no matter how profoundly our children are affected by autism, this syndrome cannot take away our ability to choose to live splendidly. Our son, Franke, will probably remain severely limited by his autistic symptoms, yet there is happiness in our day-to-day activities and eager anticipation for the future. We never, ever stop hoping that one day Franke will be able to speak his name.[23]

As you face the challenge of raising a child with autism, remember God is with you, and He is your strength. This is why He says, "Never will I leave you; never will I forsake you" (Heb. 13:5). That is a reliable promise.

Chapter 3

PARENTING PERSEVERANCE

F ROM BIRTH TO college, every step along my journey represented a constant challenge for my parents as they discovered the skills required to raise a child with autism and learning disabilities. An ancient Chinese proverb teaches, "A journey of a thousand miles must begin with a single step." I would see the wisdom of that statement when my family and I hit the kind of roadblock that was beyond our resources and control. Only if God provided a miracle would I be able to accomplish His purpose for my life.

It happened in the middle of my junior year of high school in 1993–94. I felt strong and on top of the world; my life was on track. I had committed my life to serving Christ and chose friends with strong moral values and goals. I made the honor roll two straight quarters, was a star athlete in track and cross-country, and had memorized more than two thousand scriptures. I felt the blessing and favor of God on my life, a living example of the psalm that says: "Surely, LORD, you bless the righteous; you surround them with your favor as with a shield" (Ps. 5:12).

In the spring of 1994 our 3,200-meter relay team finished twelfth in the Michigan state track meet. As we drove back from Midland, the star anchor on our relay team commented to our coach, "Next year we could be the fastest 3,200-meter relay team in the state, but Ron will be past the age requirement!"

Just then I sensed God speaking to my heart: "If you don't run on the team, no one will, for I will make a way for you to run." Looking at them, I said, "God will provide a way for me to compete next year."

"There have been many other athletes past the age requirements that have sued the MHSAA (Michigan High School Athletic Association)," the coach replied with a laugh, "and every one of them has failed!"

My age problem originated years earlier, when I had to repeat kindergarten because of learning disabilities and lack of communication skills. Yet my parents believed in God's promise that spring—that He would create a way for me to run. We prayed daily for that miracle. After all, as one of the fastest 800-meter runners in the state, I was a natural for a track and field scholarship. Yet, as my senior year approached, Mom contacted the high school athletic director and the MHSAA. Both responded: "Due to your son being three months past the age requirement, we will not allow him to compete. This is the one rule of eligibility for which we never make an exception!" My parents contacted various attorneys; all told them a lawsuit would cost more than $40,000—a price we simply could not afford.

STREAMS OF PROVISION

The summer preceding my senior year, I proceeded in faith and prepared for the coming season by running more than five hundred miles. However, as days turned into weeks, and the fall cross-country season drew near, the circumstances still appeared bleak. Finally my parents told me, "There's nothing we can do now but trust God and place your track season into His hands. He has seen all your hard work and determination."

After a five-mile run that June, I picked up a copy of the *Detroit Free Press*. The front page carried an article about

Craig Stanley, a fellow cross-country and track athlete. Stanley was also past the age limit. Our situations were nearly identical. Both born in May of 1975, we each repeated early elementary grades. Now we were both cross-country and track runners facing competition restrictions because of age. (Most importantly Craig and I both professed faith in Jesus Christ as our Lord and Savior.)

Mom immediately contacted the newspaper and Craig's family. We met later that week at the Stanleys' home in Grosse Pointe. After sharing our struggles with overcoming learning disabilities and our desire to compete as seniors, Craig's dad told my parents, "It will take a miracle for them to run. No attorney is willing to take these young men's cases." Undeterred, I shared what God had spoken and said, "Craig and I will run on the team; God will make a way!"[1]

After I rededicated my life to Christ as a junior, God placed a desire in heart to be baptized as a demonstration of that commitment. On Sunday, 6/10/94, Pastor Rob baptized me following the church service. As he lifted me from the water, he said, "God has given me a word for you. Joel 2:25: 'I will repay you for the years the locusts have eaten—the great locust and the young locust, the other locusts and the locust swarm—my great army that I sent among you.' God has promised your blessings will begin today, and He will repay all the years that the locusts have destroyed through your disabilities. He has something special in store for you this very day."

Afterward, when I got home, I had an unexpected message on our answering machine from a young attorney in Ann Arbor. He said he believed our case would set precedent for the Americans with Disabilities Act (ADA), and he wanted to represent our case pro bono. The next week both families met with Rick Landau at his office. He explained the significance of the ADA, passed just four years earlier, and told us he believed we could win our case.

About ten weeks after my baptism, and six hours before our first cross-country meet, a federal court judge granted a temporary restraining order to allow Craig and me to participate. Twenty days later the judge made it a permanent injunction, allowing us to compete for the rest of the season.

During a hearing on our case, the judge had told the MHSAA attorney: "There has been track and field competition before the time of the ancient Greeks, so I don't buy your argument that these two young men will destroy the sport! But I can guarantee if they are prohibited from competing, you will ruin their senior year of high school."

A Defining Moment

This experience marked a key defining moment in my life. Our 3,200-meter relay team set the school record twice and ran the second-fastest time out of 182 teams in Michigan. This same season God called me to be in ministry. Michigan Christian College (now Rochester College) awarded me an athletic scholarship for cross-country and track. My freshman year, I made the dean's list both semesters and received an academic scholarship to Oral Roberts University.

Athletics made a tremendous difference in my development of social skills and confidence. I learned from my teammates how to interact in social situations and found the motivation to succeed in life. Those qualities enabled me to graduate summa cum laude with a bachelor's degree in practical ministry and a master of divinity with high honors and a perfect 4.0 GPA. I felt like Eric Liddell, the Olympic track athlete portrayed in *Chariots of Fire*, who declared, "I believe God made me for a purpose, but He also made me fast. And when I run I feel His pleasure."[2]

In raising an ASD son or daughter, you will also experience situations beyond your control that will require the grace and power of God. There is no blueprint or master plan to parenting a child with a disability. It requires love, patience, faith, and dedication. In this chapter I will review methods to help you to raise your child to interact in society, develop skills, and thrive. As my track testimony demonstrates, the first steps in raising a child with autism are to commit your child to the Lord and fight hard for him or her to succeed.

Kristine Barnett is the mother of an ASD teenager whose son, Jacob, has an IQ higher than Einstein's and became a paid researcher at the age of twelve. In her book, *The Spark*, she wrote, "Whenever I meet an autistic kid who has made progress, I know that someone fought hard for that kid. No matter what the accomplishment—whether he's toilet trained or in secondary school, whether he's recently started talking again or has gotten his first job, I know that someone behind that child believed in him and that they fought for him."[3]

Only God is able to handle every situation your child will experience. During his life, legendary evangelist Oral Roberts (who inspired me during my ORU studies) liked to tell his supporters how God makes the impossible possible, even in impossible situations. Likewise, God has created your son or daughter for a special purpose, one only he or she can fulfill. As 1 Peter 4:10 states, "Each of you should use whatever gift you have received to serve others, as faithful stewards of God's grace in its various forms."

TRANSFORM A SPECIAL INTEREST

Temple Grandin, the author with autism I mentioned previously, says in her book that about fifty thousand people with ASD turn eighteen every year in the United States alone:

That's a little late to be thinking about adulthood. I tell parents that by the time their ASD kids are eleven or twelve, the parents should be thinking about what the kids are going to do when they grow up. Nobody needs to make a final decision at that point, but the parents should start considering the possibilities so that they have time to help prepare the child.[4]

In an interview Rhonda Gelstein, the mother of a child with ASD, told me how doctors had warned her that the odds of her baby's survival were less than 20 percent and to be prepared for the worst.[5] Born with cerebral palsy and autism, Rhonda's son, Tyler Laviolette, weighed just one pound, five ounces at birth and required acute care for a hundred days. Despite her son's severe disabilities, Rhonda burned with the determination to help Tyler live a normal life and be independent—a dream that would come true. To realize it, she provided her son unconditional love, support, and daily help with studies.

As a child, Tyler loved to return cans with his mom at the supermarket for a refund. He watched with amazement as the roller machine crushed the cans, just like the monster truck, "Bigfoot," smashed over cars. During Tyler's senior year of high school, his mom visited a post-secondary program for students with disabilities. Under Michigan law, students with disabilities are entitled to public education until age twenty-six. After Rhonda's visit, she went home and cried bitterly, horrified over what she had seen. Adults with great talents and potential instead received babysitting services, as if they were little children. Rhonda told her husband, "I'll create a program—if I have to—before I put my son in a program like that!"

Through hard work, determination, and his parents' continual support, Tyler graduated from high school in 2011. Afterward he searched for employment for three years without a hint of success. Meanwhile his mom contemplated the things that interested Tyler, in hopes he might develop one into gainful employment. The idea that kept coming to mind was Tyler's love of returning cans. So, in August of 2013, Rhonda helped her son start Tyler's Bottle Service and obtain resources from a community services agency (just two months after he graduated from Michigan Career and Technical Institute).

The program provided Tyler's business with a part-time driver to take him to pick up bottles and cans and return them. Tyler's business flourished, returning more than twelve thousand cans and bottles in its initial three-month period. With clients in eight cities and two counties, his record haul amounted to more than one thousand cans in ten gigantic bags. All this activity eventually prompted an expansion, with the agency providing an additional ten hours of driving assistance so Tyler could work five days a week.

"Tyler's business is a total God thing," Rhonda told me. "He is currently mentoring a young man from Bay City who has a seizure and heart condition, teaching him to build his own bottles and cans company."

FOCUS ON GIFTEDNESS

The gifted Jacob Barnett, whom I mentioned earlier, was diagnosed with moderate to severe autism at the age of two. Doctors, educators, and therapists warned his parents, Kristine and Michael, that this future Einstein would likely never talk or read, not even be able to tie his shoelaces or live independently. They suggested that Jacob be placed in a special education program that focused on teaching disabled children the most basic skills. One doctor said, "You won't have to worry about Jacob learning the alphabet because he never will be able to talk!"

By the age of twelve months Jacob often sat quietly, meticulously lining up his Matchbox cars in a perfectly straight line while using his finger to make sure he used exact spacing. He pointed at objects and cuddled like a typical toddler. Yet two months later Jacob's behavior digressed rapidly; he quit talking and smiling. When Kristine and Michael tickled him, he did not laugh as before. Captivated by light, shadows, and geometric shapes, his fascination with these things and regression in communication caused his parents to seek professional help.

By age two Jacob had completely quit talking. However, he carried around alphabet flash cards and would sleep with them, as if the cards were a baby blanket. He constantly stared at moving shadows on the wall—stars or plaid patterns on sofa fabric—and withdrew into his own world. Professional developmental specialists agreed that Kristine and Michael had to help Jacob learn basic skills through therapy while curtailing his distractive interests in shadows and patterns.

Determined to help Jacob enjoy life and be involved in ordinary activities, Kristine replied, "Why concentrate on what Jacob can't do? Why not focus on what he can do?"

So, against the advice of experts and her husband's wishes, Kristine followed her maternal instincts and removed him from special education to prepare him for mainstream kindergarten classes. Slowly, through his mom's support and unconditional love, Jacob began to communicate again and departed from his isolated world.

At age three he amazed his family and friends with his ability to recite every license plate in the Walmart parking lot. He astonished his mom by arranging crayons in a rainbow formation of the color spectrum. Kristine recognized her son's extraordinary gifts—and knew they would help change the world. So she encouraged Jacob to develop his unique interests. By now on board, her husband helped transform their in-house day care into a learning center for children with learning disabilities. Neighbors, business owners, and friends donated supplies for children's activities. Students built everything from cardboard castles and a universe with tinfoil stars to papier-mâché butterflies.

Kristine encouraged her son and the other children in her day care to harness their gifts and special interests, and (most importantly) to have fun. She discovered that Jacob—like many other children with ASD—loved the sensation of being squished. So Michael created a special pouch to hang from their ceiling for squishing. This sling device helped Jacob to focus on his studies and games. As Kristine and Michael had prayed and hoped, by age five Jacob could read and was ready for mainstream kindergarten.

Harnessing your child's passions causes his or her other skills to progress. Take a girl, Lauren, who was not interested in academic pursuits, like reading or counting. However, she loved to play house at day care. Kristine decided to harness Lauren's interest by teaching her the art of making pastries. At eleven, Lauren was volunteering at a soup kitchen on weekends and earning straight A's in school. This demonstrates Kristine's motto: "We meet children where they are in order to get them where they need to be."[6]

JACOB'S PLACE

Thanks to his parents' support and love, Jacob continued to advance. At four he had memorized a driving atlas of the United States and could give his parents directions from their home in Indianapolis to Chicago. Equipped with a school textbook, in just two weeks he taught himself calculus. Years later, on an episode of *60 Minutes*, then-twelve-year-old Jacob was seen being tested by a researcher of child prodigies. Jacob was given twenty-eight of the fifty states in random order, and he could immediately recite the list in precise order forward and backward. Three months later *60 Minutes* correspondent

Morley Safer asked him to repeat the order of the states given to him, and he did so perfectly.

Jacob's IQ of 170 on the Wechsler Fundamentals scale is believed to be higher than Einstein's. His amazing IQ empowered him to take college classes at age eight and graduate from Indiana University–Purdue University Indianapolis at twelve. At fourteen he held his master's degree, was studying for a PhD in quantum physics, and had published scientific research articles. Jacob invests his free time tutoring students in calculus. "Jacob always had a preternaturally acute ability to detect patterns," wrote his mom. "And this, of all his gifts, was the attribute the professors he'd been studying with always singled out as the key ingredient to his success."[7]

Such gifts have attracted the attention of academics like Dr. Joanne Ruthsatz, a psychology professor at Ohio State University who has researched the connection of autism and child prodigies. In a phone interview she attributed Jacob's exceptional memory to his ability to internalize facts and concepts by fluid intelligence and working memory rather than crystallized intelligence.[8] Examples of fluid intelligence are your ability to know how to swim, or ride a bike. An example of crystallized intelligence is your ability to recall your wife's or child's birth dates.

In a statement she commented, "Our findings suggest child prodigies have traits in common with autistic children, but something is preventing them from displaying the deficits we associate with the disorder.... Prodigies may have some moderated form of autism that actually enables their extraordinary talent."[9] In an interview she later stated, "And so I believe there's a genetic modifier that is holding back the deficits and allowing that talent to shine through."[10]

The possibilities of such achievement inspired Kristine Barnett to establish a charity. Jacob's Place helps children with ASD and other learning disabilities to reach their full potential through sports and fun activities. Its mission statement: "To enhance the lives of children on the autism spectrum, through social groups, maximizing skills and talents, and just plain fun!" As Kristine encourages parents, "If you fuel a child's innate spark, it will always point the way to far greater heights than you could ever have imagined."[11]

PROACTIVE

This section and the next were written by my mom, Janet Sandison, a professional artist and stay-at-home-mom.

Ron's development in infancy appeared normally. He giggled, pointed at objects, and displayed secure attachment. Ron spoke his first word, "mom," at nine months. He quickly developed a vast vocabulary of words by a year and a half. At eighteen months Ron began to regress rapidly and lost his ability to pronounce certain syllables. He quit having good eye contact and became isolated in his own world. Twenty percent of parents of children with autism report the rapid or gradual loss of words. The child then seems less interested in social interaction.[12] We had his hearing tested, and it was found to be normal.

In 1982, as Ron entered kindergarten, special education was archaic and very limited. The neuropsychological testing had only recently been formulated. Most insurances and counties did not cover the $900 price for neuropsychological testing. The federal government required public schools to provide public education for every child, including special education children. In response to federal laws, the public special education programs in Oakland County would unfairly label most students with learning disabilities as emotionally impaired. The reason the public school system did this was to keep special education cost-effective while still providing the required accommodations for students with disabilities.

This format for special education caused many children to be misdiagnosed and not to receive the proper help required for their unique disabilities. Children in special education, with their varying disabilities, from dyslexia, autism, mental delays, and other handicaps, were all grouped together in one classroom. In her book, *Martian in the Playground*, Clare Sainsbury wrote, "Mixing children together with a great variety of special needs could also expose children with Asperger's to possible manipulation and victimtization by emotionally and behaviorally disturbed children."[13]

The "emotionally impaired" diagnosis implied that the child's emotions rather than his or her neurological processes were the underlying cause of developmental delay. This misdiagnosis demonstrated that the education specialists, due to their lack of resources and ability to test properly, were hindered from determining a child's disabilities. Due to this system, at age seven Ron was mislabeled "emotionally impaired." Later testing confirmed that Ron's disabilities involved neurological processing and were not psychological. The public education system's habit of labeling children "emotionally impaired" caused them to suffer social stigma and lack of self-esteem. I could tell that my son's main learning disabilities were auditory and neurological in nature.

When Ron was misdiagnosed, I told the education specialists and his teachers, "If you are unable to properly determine what my son's disability is, in the fall I will pay for neurological testing and tell you."

After the neurological testing, Ron was officially diagnosed with auditory input disability (PDD-NOS). This learning disability hampers written expression and auditory processing abilities. In his evaluation, neuropsychologist Dr. Jerel E. Deldotto stated: "Ronald has a significant psycholinguistic deficit. This deficit was generally apparent across all basic receptive language tests, where he had difficulty in discriminating, blending, segmenting, and matching sounds. It was also apparent in his expressive language abilities, as he had difficulty repeating words, generating words with particular sounds, and naming common objects. The nature of these performances suggests that Ronald's deficits are related to a failure to understand the phonological or acoustical structure of language."

My proactive approach helped Ron to receive the testing required to diagnose his learning disability. Once we had an understanding of his learning disability, we were able to provide him with treatment and tutors. This extra support helped him to develop social skills and overcome his unique disabilities. As a parent of a child with ASD, you need to be proactive with your son or daughter's education and treatment plan. Your support and advocacy will help your child to receive the therapy and services required to overcome his or her unique disability.

DEVELOPING YOUR CHILD'S GIFTS

Dr. Temple Grandin has said that in special education, there's too much emphasis placed on the deficits and not enough on the strengths. At age four Ron already demonstrated a flair for art and writing. One of his favorite activities was dictating short fictional stories about his stuffed animals and drawing illustrations. I wrote Ron's short stories in spiral notebooks. Ron drew the main characters Chatter the Squirrel, Little Gnawing Beaver, Bouncing Bear, and Prairie Pup. I was able to teach Ron new vocabulary through writing, which also helped his imagination to blossom. By watching me write, Ron learned reading comprehension and memorized the spelling of words.

When Ron was in fourth grade, his teacher had the class enter the Detroit Edison Safety Poster Contest. Ron drew Prairie Pup building a fort near electrical lines with the warning, "Don't build forts too close to the power lines!" This drawing won an award for the ten-year-old age group in Oakland County. For the grand prize Ron and Prairie Pup met NBA Hall of Famer and Detroit Pistons all-time points and assists leader Isiah Thomas. Overnight Prairie Pup was an instant local celebrity as Isiah patted him on the head. Through writing and artwork, my son was able to develop self-esteem and social skills. The girls in Ron's classes created outfits for the beloved Prairie Pup. This interaction helped give Ron confidence when speaking with girls from an early age. From kindergarten through fifth grade Ron always carried a book in his right hand and Prairie Pup in his left.

My writing creative stories with Ron has made him curious about the world, and he became an avid reader. During the past decade Ron has read more than nine hundred books, written three books, and had many articles published. I helped further his quest for knowledge by spending time with him, writing stories, and encouraging him to read. By the eighth grade Ron was attending all regular education classes and once again had a vast vocabulary.

No Man's Valley

At the age of six I developed an obsession for Laura McCarley's children's book, *Welcome to No Man's Valley*, and the animated film based on the book. Every night before bed I would read this short book and watch the half-hour video. The story line follows a California condor who goes on an adventure to find Utopia, a place where extinct and endangered species can live safely, away from the dangers of humans.

In my room I built my version of No Man's Valley, fashioned

by covering a coffee table with a blanket. On top of the table I placed a moving animal train and a watchtower composed of LEGOs. This utopia came complete with Prairie Pup (the mayor) and all my other favorite critters. When I felt fear or anxiety, I entered No Man's Valley through its blanket door and felt calm. No Man's Valley was a stress-free environment where I could go and teach myself to read and write my creative animal adventures. If anyone touched No Man's Valley or moved the animals from their exact place, I would throw a tantrum.

My mom joked, "I kept having nightmares that Ronnie's No Man's Valley would move out from his room and take over the whole house." It is not uncommon for a child with autism to invent such a device to relieve stress.

When Temple Grandin was in college, she invented a squeeze chute to help her overcome autism. She designed her human chute after those used for cattle. This chute provided her relief from panic attacks while stimulating her mind for thinking and studying. Many children with ASD will create a special area where they can relax and experience freedom from anxiety. My creation of No Man's Valley enabled my imagination and creativity to blossom. The themes from the book and movie were concepts that helped me overcome my learning disabilities.

To illustrate, here is some dialogue between the elder/chief California condor and the younger condor, Elliot, which encourages children:

> There is a place far, far away where endangered and existent animals can go safe from the problems of the outside world. It's called No Man's Valley. All I know, is to reach it, you must have faith and the will to survive, endurance beyond belief and the courage to overcome hardship, terror, and obstacles too horrible to describe. Only you can fly there and complete the journey.[14]

Steps to Helping Your Child

Here are some steps you should take when your child is diagnosed with autism.

Provide a strong support group of families and friends.

You cannot help your child if your own life is falling apart. This network of supporters will give you the strength and encouragement to move forward. An autism support group can help you meet other families who are struggling with similar challenges. You can share information, get advice, and lean on each other for emotional support.

Provide stability and care for your child.

Do this through consistency, setting a fixed schedule, praising positive behavior, creating your home as a safe haven—and especially prayer. Be consistent; children with ASD have difficulty adapting to new situations and environments. If you are consistent in applying the information your child is taught in school and at therapy sessions, it helps reinforce the skills he or she has learned. My mom accomplished this by having me include in my creative stories the subjects I was learning in school. As Dr. Laura Henderson wrote:

> Once a ritual is established with a spectrum kid, it attracts him just as strongly as the negative behavior once did, because he finds repetition comforting....Taking a child's hand or shoulders and walking him through the steps of obedience at the same time you tell him what to do will increase the likelihood that he'll understand and obey.[15]

Keep to a fixed schedule.

Children with autism tend to thrive in a highly structured routine. Have a schedule with regular times for meals, school, therapy, showering, and bedtime. If your child's schedule has to be altered, tell him or her in advance.

Praise positive behavior.

When your child demonstrates good behavior, offer him or her positive reinforcement by praising proper actions. Be specific about the behavior you are praising. Reward your child for such behavior with his or her favorite candy, stickers, video game, ice cream, or toys.

Make your home a safe haven.

ASD children need a safe place to go when they feel anxious or afraid. This safe zone can be a fort in the basement, a doll house, or a library. Make sure to remove any items from your home that might harm your child during a tantrum or meltdown.

Pray continually for your child's protection and future.

The Apostle Paul wrote, "Pray continually" (1 Thess. 5:17). My mom prayed without ceasing that God would provide me with a beautiful and godly wife who could be my ministry companion. She prayed and believed that God would give me a Proverbs 31 wife: "Her husband [Ron] has full confidence in her and lacks nothing of value. She brings him [Ron] good, not harm, all the days of her life" (Prov. 31:11–12). You can pray this prayer for your child by inserting your child's name into these verses.

In college, my mom would send me money once a month with a postscript: "P.S., use this money to take a nice Christian girl out on a date." She encouraged me through her prayers and gifts to have confidence to ask girls out and be social. Many young men and women with autism lack self-confidence and never develop the social skills required for dating and marriage. My mom's prayers and persistence paid off, and God provided me with Kristen, a beautiful, godly wife.

Provide fun games and activities for your child.

Games and activities will help your son or daughter interact with peers, develop social skills, and discover new interests. It is worth remembering these words from author Stuart Brown: "The toys of today become the technology of tomorrow."[16] In a similar vein, Lisa Jo Rudy, whose son Tom has ASD, encourages parents:

> When kids with autism get out into the real world, they find people, places, programs, activities, and interests they'd never have experienced in the closed box of therapies and schools. Sometimes those interests grow into volunteer opportunities or internships—in some cases, careers and relationships can result. Perhaps even more important, parents and siblings desperately need the sense of community that they are denied when children with autism are part of the family....
>
> Only by getting out into the wide world can a parent see his child overcome an obstacle and rise to a challenge such as running the bases, performing on stage, or winning a merit badge. And only by allowing a child with autism to experience the world can a parent discover a child's unexpected talent in art, music, science, or athletics.[17]

Trust your child to God's care by taking each day at a time.

Jesus said, "Therefore do not worry about tomorrow, for tomorrow will worry about itself. Each day has enough trouble of its own" (Matt. 6:34). Joni Parsley, wife of pastor Rod Parsley of World Harvest Church in Columbus, Ohio—whose son, Austin, has Asperger's—once said, "If you look at five years from now and wonder if you'll still be dealing with [autism], it's overwhelming. So [Rod and I] just say: 'Today, this is what's before us. And sufficient for today are the cares of today.'"[18]

Don't get overwhelmed by your fears, real or imagined, either. Consider the joys author Kelly Langston described in an article about the autism journey of her son, Alec:

I have learned to lean on God—*hard*—to get us through the difficult days. I have learned to LOOK UP to God instead of looking at my circumstances. And I find that after all of the trials, year after year and minute by minute, *we have survived.* God has proven that He is faithful. That we can still laugh. We can still smile. With dirt on our faces, standing in the muck of life, we can see with our own eyes that life is precious and holy…when God is in control.[19]

Special-Needs Moms: A Look Inside

As we near the close of this chapter, I want to share a poem written by April Vernon, the mother of a special-needs child:

You may think us "special moms" have it pretty rough.
We have no choice. We just manage life when things
   get really tough.
We've made it through the days we thought we'd never
   make it through.
We've even impressed our own selves with all that we
   can do.

We've gained patience beyond measure, love we never
   dreamed of giving.
We worry about the future, but know this "special" life
   is worth living.
We have bad days and hurt sometimes, but we hold our
   heads up high.
We feel joy and pride and thankfulness more often
   than we cry.

For our kids, we aren't just supermoms. No, we do so
   much more.
We are cheerleaders, nurses, and therapists who don't
   walk out the door.

We handle rude remarks and unkind stares with
    dignity and grace.
Even though the pain they bring cannot be erased.

Therapies and treatment routes are a lot for us to digest.
We don't know what the future holds but give our kids
    our best.
None of us can be replaced, so we don't get many
    breaks.
It wears us out, but to help our kids we'll do whatever
    it takes.

We are selfless, not by choice you see. Our kids just
    have more needs.
We're not out to change the world, but we want to plant
    some seeds.
We want our kids accepted. That really is our aim.
When we look at them we just see kids. We hope you'll
    do the same.[20]

Summary

While parenting a son or daughter with autism can be a challenge, it also can offer great joy as you see your child refine his unique gifts and follow the call of God. As you have learned, the key to success is helping your child to become involved in fun activities while focusing on his strengths. These strengths and gifts will empower him to overcome disabilities and develop skills that are useful in the workplace. As you apply these principles, your child—like Tyler Laviolette, Jacob Barnett, and me—will be prepared for the long journey ahead. In the next chapter you will learn how to choose a mentor for your child and the benefits of mentoring offers.

Chapter 4

MENTORING

A S YOUNG CHILDREN and throughout high school, my brother Chuck and I had a cat named Mitzi and pet mice. We can still name and describe every pet mouse we had over the years: Mousy (white fur, red eyes), Fred and Ralph (twin brothers; big, brown fur), Sparkie and Spunky (a father and son with a mixture of white and black fur and each with a black patch over one eye), Zimie (white fur, red eyes), Satin (overweight, black fur), and Bungle (a wild field mouse, brown fur with soft, white belly).

At fourteen years of age Mitzi was still a mighty hunter. She lived twenty-two human years and even caught a baby rabbit on Easter the year before she died. One warm summer night Chuck heard a loud squeaking noise in our living room. He ran to the dark moonlit room just in time to discover Mitzi preparing to bounce on a defenseless, tiny field mouse that was covering her face with her paws. Chuck quickly grabbed the field mouse and gently placed her in a cage. Then, he named the little ball of fur Bungle.

Unlike our other furry friends, Bungle was far from tame. She nipped at others, attempted to escape from the cage, and refused to be held. One Christmas when I came home from college on break, Chuck and I got the crazy idea of trying to tame Bungle. We decided to have two female companions from a pet store mentor this "wild kingdom" mouse. We thought these tame mice, Cinnamon and Charcoal, could act as missionaries to Bungle and help transform her.

At first, this plan proved a failure. Bungle would snarl at Cinnamon and Charcoal. If they were feeling daring and got too close, she would not hesitate to bite. Late at night Bungle would sneak into Cinnamon and Charcoal's nest, which consisted of toilet paper and wood chips. Bungle would quickly steal the toilet paper blankets and hide them in the bottom of the cage. After Bungle's blanket theft, Cinnamon and Charcoal would huddle close to keep warm.

One freezing winter night everything changed. Bungle, as usual, stole the toilet paper and went to her nest below. She was lying comfortably in the blankets when she heard Cinnamon and Charcoal shivering. That touched Bungle's heart. She carried the blankets from her secret stash, climbed the tunnel to the top, and brought the blankets to Cinnamon and Charcoal. All three slept that night cuddled together in one big ball of fur. The three mice became best friends and inseparable.

Cinnamon and Charcoal helped transform Bungle from a member of the wild kingdom to the province of tame mice. After her conversion, Bungle no longer bit her companions or stole their blankets and food. In a perfect parallel to human relationships, they mentored Bungle in proper etiquette. As such, mentoring can help your ASD child learn social skills, hygiene, and how to develop his or her talents for the workplace.

WHEN IS YOUR BIRTHDAY?

As I printed pages of my book for editing at the library, I noticed a middle-aged gentleman with disheveled, graying hair. He approached tables with high school students, busily engaged in their group class projects and said, "Hi, Jill, 8/17/93; Hi, Kim, 6/21/92; Hi, Dan, 1/4/92..." and so forth. For each person he met, he would quote the day, year, and month of their birth date. The student librarian told me, "Jim is a special guy. If you give him your birth date, he can tell you what day of the week you were born. I am 5/6/90. The library is Jim's second home. He is here every day, playing on the computers and talking to random people."

I could instantly tell Jim was on the autism spectrum and had a savant-like gift for calendar counting and math. Kristen and I introduced ourselves to Jim. With fast, hyper-verbal, childlike speech, Jim said, "Kristen and Ron, when are your birth dates?"

Kristen replied, "3/6/82." Jim bobbed his head twice, and said, "You were born on a Saturday."

I said, "My birthday is 5/10/75." Again Jim bobbed his head twice and exclaimed, "You, like your beautiful wife, Kristen, were born on a Saturday. That's good luck!"

I noticed Jim's computer had two window screens open—one played a washing machine video, and the second a video game. So I asked, "Why do you constantly have the washing machine video playing?"

"It helps me stay calm," he replied. "I also have a Hoover vacuum cleaner video I play. As a child, I would watch the washing machine spinning, back and forth, for hours. I loved to watch my mom use the Hoover vacuum, which broke 2/13/70. Where are you from?" Jim asked.

"Bloomfield Hills," Kristen answered.

"I hate the area of 14 Mile and Southfield Road," he said. "On 4/25/74 [a Thursday] some children from Bloomfield cracked jokes at Jim. I was upset."

As Kristen and I bade Jim good-bye, I thought, "Man, Jim has an amazing gift for math and numbers but no way to harness his gift. I wonder how different life for Jim could have been if only he had received early intervention for his autism and some good therapy, and had a caring mentor to teach him social skills. His amazing gift is like an outdated calculator in the age of computers. With mentoring and therapy, Jim may have been a great professor of physics or a computer engineer. Instead, Jim is viewed by teenagers as the odd man at the library or *Rain Man's* cousin. What if my parents would not have nurtured my gifts, and I did not have mentors, tutors, and educators invest in me? Could I have become a library oddity?"

This is one reason I am eternally grateful for the mentors who helped me become more than most people thought I could achieve. Another ASD figure who shares my appreciation is a previously mentioned author, Temple Grandin. In her book *Emergence: Labeled Autistic* she described the positive impact her mentor and teacher, William Carlock, had on her life:

> Mr. Carlock didn't see any of the labels, just the under-lying talents. Even the principal had doubts about my fin-ishing tech school. But Mr. Carlock believed in building what was within the student. He channeled my fixations into constructive projects. He didn't try to draw me into his world but came instead into my world....
>
> Mr. Carlock aroused my interest in science and directed my fixation into a worthy project. I spent hours at the library looking up everything I could find on the effect sensory input into one sense system had on sensory perception in another sensory system. To my amazement I discovered that there was a whole field of study called sensory interaction. Eventually, my under-graduate thesis was concerned with sensory interaction and experiments.[1]

Choosing a Mentor

Years ago the prophet Amos posed the question: "Do two walk together unless they have agreed to do so?" (Amos 3:3). When helping your son or daughter to choose a mentor, be sure that your child enjoys and feels comfortable with that person. A mentor can be a close friend, an older student, Sunday school teacher, church elder, athletic coach, Boy Scout leader, Girl Scout leader, educator, or just someone who shares your child's common interests. When allowing someone to mentor your child, first do a background check to make sure the person has no criminal record and is otherwise "safe." Parents should be involved in the mentoring process and receive feedback from the mentor on their child's progress. Feedback from the child is helpful to be sure they are compatible.

Susan Osborne, workplace readiness director of Autism Works Now, told me, "For mentoring to be effective, it must be fun for both child and mentor. Some fun activities can include outings to the zoo, museums, movies, art fair, park, beach, campground, sports event, coffee shop, or restaurant, or long walks and bike rides. During such activities the mentor can help teach your child social skills, managing emotions, controlling stress, and how to enjoy life to a greater extent."[2]

Divine Connection

In the middle of my junior year in high school I dedicated my life to serving Christ. At this time the Holy Spirit placed it on my heart to memorize the Bible. I took the words of King David seriously: "I have hidden your word in my heart that I might not sin against you" (Ps. 119:11). It wasn't enough to know it, though. I wanted to follow the words of the legendary evangelist, D. L. Moody: "The Scriptures were *not given to increase our knowledge, but* to transform our lives."[3]

As I served Christ first, it transformed my life. I quit swearing and stopped hanging around negative peers and environments. In their place, I focused on three things— memorizing the Scriptures, track and cross-country, and academics. In less than a year I had memorized more than two thousand scriptures.

When I shared my testimony and preached at youth events, people kept saying, "You have the scriptures memorized just like Dr. Jack Van Impe." In those pre-Internet days when I couldn't google for an answer, I would reply, "Who's Dr. Jack Van Impe?" One Sunday night as I flipped quickly through the TV stations, I decided to stop on the channel where Van Impe and his wife, Rexella, were teaching about eschatology and Christ's return. I was amazed at his extraordinary Bible knowledge and that he could quote Scripture from memory with such authority. I figured his ministry was probably based in California or Texas. At the conclusion of the program the announcer noted that the following week the ministry would have its first-ever open house where the public could met the Van Impes and the rest of their team. I was stunned to learn his office and studio were less than ten minutes from our house.

A week later I met them and shared my testimony, telling Jack how I had memorized thousands of verses. Before this, I had memorized passages by books of the Bible; I didn't have them on index cards, just highlighted in my Bible. He taught me how to memorize by subject and write the verses on three-by-five-inch cards. He also shared his special memorization methods. At the end of our conversation he invited me to apply to be a summer intern.

The summer of my senior year at ORU (1999) I served as an intern for Van Impe's ministry. Through this internship I learned the skills required for operating an international ministry and developed my ministry skills. One of the ways he mentored me was by sharing about his experiences in his early days as a traveling evangelist and how the Lord provided for him as he was establishing the ministry.

This gracious couple even invited me to a live taping of

their program, *Dr. Jack Van Impe Presents.* While filming, he was quoting Bible verses when suddenly he gently tapped his hands against his forehead, out of frustration, and exclaimed, "I lost my train of thought. I just can't remember the reference for that verse!" I smiled and said to his director, "The verses are Psalm 8:2 and Matthew 21:16, 'From the lips of children and infants you have ordained praise.'" The director laughed, amused at the fact that I immediately knew the references.

This experience proved to be another defining moment in my life. It helped me develop self-confidence and learn the crucial skills for working with others. Dr. Van Impe also taught me the importance of faith and integrity in ministry. More than a decade has passed since he gave me advice about my future that burned an indelible mark in my mind. He said if I desired to be effective in ministry, I should look for a wife like Rexella, someone who always believed in me and shared my passion for Christ.

Like Rexella, Kristen is a woman of faith who believes in me and God's visions for my life. Internships with mentors in your son's or daughter's area of interest and expertise can offer great opportunities for them to learn skills for the workplace and connections for the future. Most individuals' career paths and employment are paved through relationships and friendships.

MENTORING QUALITIES

The most important qualities for a mentor of children with autism and special needs are patience, consistency, flexibility, and understanding. Without patience, a mentor will not be able to handle a child with autistic quirks and repetitive behavior patterns. Consistency is required for your child to trust the mentor to be on time for his or her visits. If a mentor makes plans with your son and fails to call in case of a change of plans, this can have a devastating emotional impact.

A mentor also needs to be flexible and understand your child's obsessions. Julie Ann Reed, whose son has Asperger's, said, "If your son or daughter has an obsession, use it to help him to learn new material. My son Paul is obsessed with computers, so I use computers as a reward system."[4]

Check with social service agencies and your local school district and see if they offer any mentoring program or one-to-one assistance. Mentoring needs to begin with the most basic skills, such as hygiene. I learned the importance of hygiene at Oral Roberts University in Tulsa, Oklahoma. During my time on campus ORU had an open house twice a semester, when students were allowed to visit each other's dorms for three hours. This particular day the thermometer had surpassed 100 degrees. A number of women glistened with sweat as they headed toward the men's dorms. I was in a hurry too, having forgotten to make my bed and clean my room prior to the open house. Two beautiful women stood next to me as I waited anxiously for the elevator door to open. By the time it creaked into sight, five more girls were in line.

There I stood, surrounded by beautiful women wearing their ORU-mandated dresses. It felt like heaven on earth until I heard the women giggling. Suddenly an awful smell hit my nostrils, a stench I compare to crayfish decomposing in a hot garage for two weeks. Horrified, I looked around to see a familiar sight: Donald. Standing in the middle of the elevator, he was dressed in a filthy, sweat-covered, oversized "mad flasher" trench coat. His greasy hair hadn't been washed or combed the whole semester (maybe the past decade). The two girls standing by my side whispered to each other, "Look, it's the mad scientist from the 1980s movies!"

Looking Donald in the eyes, I said, "Man, it is really hot

today, over 100 degrees. How can you stand to wear your three-piece suit, tie, and a trench coat? You must be roasting!"

Fidgeting with his hands, Donald looked down as he wiped sweat from his chin and replied, "I don't feel too hot today!" The girls continued to giggle in the background.

I had seen Donald previously in the computer lab located in the men's dorm. He had been dressed in the same dirty suit and trench coat. A buddy told me Donald was in the computer lab 24/7 playing video games and listening to Beatles music, and when he leaves the computer keypad stinks to high heaven! One of Donald's former roommates said he had marked Donald's shampoo bottle with a red marker the second week of school, and the amount of shampoo never decreased.

I later learned that Donald had been a full-time student living on campus at ORU for sixteen years. He had already earned about eight degrees, ranging from computer science and biology to theology. When he entered ORU in 1984, the cost of tuition was around $2,500, and it was a set tuition. So the price never increased. Rather than finding a facility where someone could help take care of him, which can be costly, Donald had remained in the structured environment of college.

"He is a smart guy but has horrible hygiene and absolutely zero people skills. He could never survive on his own without help."

Like Donald, many young adults and children with autism struggle with daily hygiene. A mentor should teach your child proper hygiene routines, such as showering, using deodorant, shaving, combing hair, brushing teeth, washing clothes, and keeping his or her room clean.

These skills are essential for the workplace and developing friendships.

MATTERS OF FAITH

After a mentor helps your child develop good hygiene prac-
tices, the mentor should help him or her develop a walk of
faith. As the Apostle Paul said, "The spiritual did not come
first, but the natural, and after that the spiritual" (1 Cor. 15:46).
The writer of Hebrews advised, "Remember your leaders, who
spoke the word of God to you. Consider the outcome of their
way of life and imitate their faith" (Heb. 13:7). A Christian
mentor should share his faith by showing love to your child.
Many children with autism find religion difficult to comprehend because of their concrete thinking style and literal interpretation of language. A mother blogged on Facebook:

> For the last few years I have been trying to explain God
> and Jesus to my six-year-old son, but his autism prevents
> him from comprehending metaphysical things (every-
> thing to him is super literal). Today I picked him up
> from day care and he showed me this picture he drew
> of God and him and I said, "Did you draw Jesus?' And
> he looked at me like 'duh' and said, 'Yeah. God.' I didn't
> think he would ever understand but apparently God's
> thoughts are bigger than my own...[5]

ASD children learn theological concepts best through stories,
movies, and pictures. A mentor can help autistic children grow
in the understanding of God by sitting with them in Sunday
school and explaining the lesson. In middle school, my parents
forced my brother, Chuck, and me to attend Sunday school. I
got bored listening to the teacher's lectures, typically spoken in
a monotone. Her words sounded like Charlie Brown's teacher:
"Wah wah woh wah wah." I found it hard to learn anything
when I could not understand a single word she said.

To avoid getting bored out of my mind or daydreaming
the hour away thinking of Transformers, I decided to be the

class clown. I would disrupt the class by laughing and yelling inappropriate comments. I cracked jokes about nerdy students and nicknamed one geeky guy "Blue Light Special" because he wore clothes from Kmart. So, the Sunday school program supervisor assigned a college-age youth worker to monitor me in class. Brian would sit next to me, explain the topics the teacher reviewed, and ask questions to make sure I understood the lessons.

A former track runner, Brian loved basketball and baseball. When it came to youth group, he encouraged me to develop friendships and participate in activities and outings. During my middle school years he planned fun activities for us at least twice a month. They included playing basketball Wednesday nights at church and taking me to see action films. Brian's faith in Christ and loving actions helped me understand the meaning of being a disciple of Christ. He also accomplished "mission impossible"—getting me to behave in Sunday school. By being a friend and providing listening ears, mentors can help children with ASD avoid the pitfall of social mistakes. When your child does or says something inappropriate, a mentor can help him or her learn from those mistakes.

The Fantastic 4

Because many children and adults with ASD lack social skills, they have a tendency to make inappropriate and hurtful comments. As a single adult, I attended church singles activities and groups to meet women. Most of the singles in the group were between the ages twenty-five and forty. A few weird guys in their fifties made occasional appearances and flirted with the younger girls. When I saw them, I would make fun of these guys openly, nicknaming the creepiest ones "The Fantastic Four," after the Marvel Comics superheroes. I tagged this particular group of misfits "Hairy Back Man," "Walker Man," "Barracuda Man," and "Dr. Stare."

At every event Hairy Back Man often wore a tank top exposing his Chia Pet–like furry chest. The top of his head was bare, with thinning black hair barely covering the sides. Along with a King James Version of the Bible, he often carried a book titled *How Not to Wreck Your Second Marriage Like the First*. Once, when Hairy Back Man cornered two blondes in their twenties, I approached him and asked, "I see you have a great book! Have you read the sequel yet, *How Not to Wreck Your Third Marriage Like the First and Second*?" The women smiled at me and giggled.

I guessed Walker Man to be in his late forties. He stood about five feet, three inches tall, and had the kind of appearance that made it seem like his head was stuck between his shoulders. (He had been in a serious auto accident.) One night, as I carried on a conversation with a woman I'll call Megan—a beautiful, six-foot-two blonde—Walker Man whirled around in his camouflage, deer-hunter T-shirt. Interrupting me in the middle of a sentence, he said, "You are one tall, beautiful girl! I used to be real tall also, about six-four before my accident."

"What happened to you?" I commented. "Did you hit a deer while driving? Wait! No deer could've possibly done that kind of collateral damage. You must have been mauled in two by a grizzly bear camping at Yellowstone Park."

Walker Man slinked away and went on to the next couple.

Barracuda Man was so aggressive in his seduction techniques and skilled in stalking that after his third warning, a singles leader told him, "We feel it is best for the group and you not to attend here. Women are really freaked out by your aggressive approach. Should you choose to come back, they will file a restraining order against you."

Three months later my friend saw Barracuda Man at the

library, hitting on the young librarians. He walked over and said, "I haven't seen you at the singles group. All the pretty girls have been asking about you: 'Where is that cool, older gentleman with the leather jacket?' These girls wished you would have asked them out also."

Barracuda Man contemplated that for a minute and replied, "Uh, the leaders told me those girls were really creeped out, and I should never come back!"

"Oh, they're just jealous that a man in his fifties, like you, is getting all the young girls!" my friend replied.

"That settles it. Next week I'll be there!"

The following week my friend and I sat in the back row and watched the leadership team escort a confused Barracuda Man from the service.

A professor in his fifties, Dr. Stare gained his name because of his standard pick-up approach: staring down young girls and telling them, "I think I met you before. My name is…" This caused them to feel uncomfortable and frightened. Soon after Kristen and I were married, we went to a book signing for best-selling author Mitch Albom. Next to us in line, hitting on a young woman, was Dr. Stare. Excitedly I said to Kristen, "There's Dr. Stare. He is one of the creepiest men on the planet! I have to go over and say something to him."

"Honey, don't make fun of him," she said. "He can't help being socially awkward, and God loves him. How would you feel if you had a serious staring problem?"

As you can tell from these anecdotes, I needed help with social graces. Kristen has encouraged me to avoid making fun of people who are a little different or weird. (Who am I to talk, right?) Many individuals with Asperger's struggle holding back comments and saying everything on their mind, no matter how inappropriate; this is a fault I have struggled to overcome. I need to remember the Apostle Paul's words to "not let any unwholesome talk come out of your mouths, but only what is helpful for building others according to their needs, that it may benefit those who listen" (Eph. 4:29).

Mentoring a child with autism requires instructing him in what is appropriate to discuss, as well as when to remain silent. In my interviews with parents of ASD children, parents of those with Asperger's said the leading hindrance to their child obtaining gainful employment is foolish things he or she says without thinking, often accompanied by a failure to recognize social settings. Unkind words spoken can lead to hurt feelings and mangled relationships.

Golden Apples

Proverbs is loaded with wisdom for life, particularly these verses:

> Pleasant words are as a honeycomb, sweet to the soul and health to the bones.
> —Proverbs 16:24, mev

> A word fitly spoken is like apples of gold in settings of silver.
> —Proverbs 25:11, mev

As a child and young adult, I was brutally honest with people and said many hurtful things. One social skill I wish a mentor would have taught me is to say pleasant words and not simply blurt out everything on my mind.

I particularly suffered from social awkwardness because of a problem with hypoglycemia from first to seventh grade. Candy and desserts caused me to become hyper-manic; if I missed a meal, and my blood sugar level was low, I would sometimes faint or pass out. In third grade, my class participated in "secret Santa," where we bought gifts for one another anonymously.

Aware of my situation, the teacher instructed the student assigned to me, "Don't give Ron any candies or sweets for his secret Santa present, but only fruits and vegetables."

The teacher divided our class into two groups. As my group reentered the room to discover our gifts, I saw Paul had a bag full of candy, Allison had five candy bars, and Rene a chocolate Santa. I looked over at my desk. There sat a big red apple. Enraged, I screamed at the top of my lungs, "What stupid, idiotic kid would give an apple for secret Santa? Whoever my secret Santa is has destroyed my holiday season. Where's my candy?"

Crying, the boy who had drawn my name said through tears, "I'm so sorry. The teacher told me never to give you candy!"

I learned from this experience that hurtful words can be devastating to others. Paul, Allison, and Rene spoke grateful words to their secret Santa, which brought joy to the givers. Their "golden apple" words were a delight to the soul, while my hurtful words resembled road apples (horse manure) by the side of the road. This is why autism researcher Dr. Lynn Koegel advises that "parents and mentors need to teach children the difference between an appropriate and inappropriate comment and practice the appropriate social conversation as frequently and in as many different contexts as possible. And be prepared to explain once in a while that you're still working on teaching your child social graces, in case there's a blunder."[6]

EMOTIONAL CHECK

Many children with ASD have difficulty controlling their emotions. Without proper training and therapy, children who lack emotional control will continue to display disruptive behavior and meltdowns. They will demonstrate the truth of this proverb: "A hot-tempered person must pay the penalty; rescue them, and you will have to do it again" (Prov. 19:19).

Dealing with this requires patience and maturity on your part. Dr. Laura Hendrickson explains:

> It's important to understand that autism spectrum anger is different from typical anger. When you get angry, there are graduations in your response. You might be a little miffed, pretty irritated, or absolutely enraged, depending on the circumstance. But your spectrum child can come completely unglued without even realizing it, until he's totally out of control, and it can happen almost instantaneously.[7]

Mentors can help teach children emotional management and the wisdom of Paul's advice: "'In your anger do not sin': Do not let the sun go down while you are still angry" (Eph. 4:26). Teaching children to properly manage their emotions enables them to get angry while avoiding an outburst or meltdown. In my life I discovered the power to control my emotions through the fruit of the Holy Spirit: "The fruit of the Spirit is love, joy, peace, forbearance, kindness, goodness, faithfulness, gentleness and self-control" (Gal. 5:22–23).

How can a mentor teach these abstract yet essential Christian concepts to a child who has difficulty interpreting nonliteral ideas or is nonverbal? The mentor (and parents) can teach the fruit of the Spirit through kind actions as they act under the influence of the Holy Spirit.

Christian theologians use two key terms for our theology and beliefs concerning the character and nature of God. The first, orthodoxy, refers to our right theology and understanding of the Creator. Due to its abstract concepts, children with autism find theology hard to understand. The second, orthopraxy, is living out our faith through our actions and lifestyle, such as helping a person in need or waiting patiently in a busy checkout line at the store. Children with autism discover faith by seeing people older than them demonstrate faith in practical ways.

Teaching emotional control requires such practical techniques as:

1. Training a child to take deep breaths as he or she experiences anxiety or anger.

2. Helping children learn to ask the teacher before going into the hall for a break from class when they feel emotions blurring their minds.

3. Instructing the child to handle being picked on by other children by immediately telling a supervising adult. ASD children need to learn to express feelings verbally to release stress.

These methods can help a child with autism to stay calm in various circumstances.

AMBER ALERT

A common media headline concerns children with autism disappearing or wandering off from their schools or homes. During the last few years I have seen numerous articles about the tragic deaths of ASD children who wandered off and drowned, or got hit by vehicles. When I was in fourth grade, a church sponsored a vacation Bible school (VBS) that met on the same street where I lived. Two hours into eight hours of the week of VBS instruction, I grew bored. So I decided to ride my bike home, just half a mile away. After eating a peanut butter sandwich, I went over to a friend's house and played video games. Knowing that VBS finished at four o'clock, I returned at 3:30 p.m. to discover the associate pastor and several teachers searching frantically for me.

As a mentor for a child with ASD, you must always be

watchful so the child does not wander. If the child has displayed this tendency, you may want to use a watch or ankle bracelet with a GPS tracking device. Author and social worker Brian King, the father of three sons on the ASD spectrum, told me, "My second son loved to wander. If you turned your back for thirty seconds, he would be gone. The best method to keep a child from wandering is get him involved in an activity he enjoys. My son loves to cook. When he is busy cooking, he doesn't wander. If you're watching a child who has a tendency to wander, have him involved in an activity that has noise, like playing video games. The sound of the game makes you know he is not wandering."[8]

Summary

A good mentor can help your child learn hygiene, management of emotions, and social skills. These qualities are essential to developing friendships and preparing him for college and employment. When you choose a mentor, make sure he or she has character, faith, patience, and understanding of your child's disability. The best mentor is a person who has the same passions and interest as your child. My experience interning under Dr. Jack Van Impe prepared me for ministry and employment. Internships can help your child develop his or her special talent and be prepared for the future.

Chapter 5

BULLY-PROOFING

S TAND BACK!" JIM shouts as he smashes a two-liter bottle of Mountain Dew on the cement. "Let's produce a video on how many hits it takes for a carbonated Dew to explode."

"Do the Dew!" John exclaims while filming his crazy friend, Jim, with his iPhone.

Crash! Bang! Thud! echo across the screen as the two-liter bottle smashes the cement like a crash car dummy four more times. Each time Jim stealthily moves back like famed crocodile hunter Steve Irwin messing with a super croc.

"Man, this two-liter's solid; it has already hit the cement five times without producing a dent," Jim says. "On the count of three, I'll use all my strength. One. Two. Three."

At the end of the count Jim hurls the two-liter over his head: *whiz, whiz, whiz.*

The torpedo soars six feet high—straight into John's face. Bang!

"It destroyed my iPhone!" a shaken John yells.

Viewers watching this scene unfold on YouTube eagerly expect crazy Jim, the two-liter smasher, to get hit by the rocket-launched Dew. Instead, it's his filming companion—John.

When children with autism are bullied frequently, they will react unpredictably. Just as the two-liter bottle hit John instead of Jim, children with ASD may lash out at someone not involved in bullying them, even a friend or teacher. Bullying can cause a sensory overload and loss of emotional control, which leads to a meltdown. They may display anger and rage toward another student or an adult not even involved in the bullying. Teasing becomes bullying when it is repetitive, or when there is a conscious intent to harm (physically or emotionally) a distressed target.

Bullies receive pleasure from watching the reaction of the person they have bullied. You can help bully-proof your child by understanding the effects of bullying and the reason bullies target ASD children, as well as recognizing the many different signs and forms of bullying. Former Michigan State basketball player Anthony Ianni's testimony of bullying, along with mine, will provide some tips to help prevent bullying and build your child's confidence.

HARMFUL EFFECTS

Bullying can negatively impact your child's self-esteem and physical and mental health. It can also lead to depression, anxiety issues, substance abuse, decreased academic achievement, peer isolation, and—in a few cases—violent outbursts or even suicide. Dr. Tony Attwood, an expert on autism, warns of the serious consequences for ASD victims:

> The psychological effects of bullying are devastating. It is a major cause of school refusal and school suspension, often because the victim has become angry and reluctantly retaliated. It can be a contributory factor in the development of an anxiety disorder, due to constant fear of bullying "attack." . . .
>
> The derogatory and provocative comments and actions may be internalized and believed by the victim, contributing to low self-esteem and a clinical depression. As so many interactions with peers are associated with being bullied, and so few positive social interactions are experienced, there can be the development of a sense of paranoia that is based on reality.[1]

HUMAN TARGET

Research shows children with disabilities are two to three times more likely to be bullied than those without a disability. Children with autism are more vulnerable due to differences in communication abilities, motor skills, and social cognition. Difficulty recognizing social cues can cause a child to appear awkward or aloof to his peers. Children with autism tend to engage in repetitive behaviors or be hypersensitive to environmental stimuli, which makes them a ripe target for bullies who hone in on differences and delight in tormenting their victims.

Hans Asperger, an Austrian pediatrician for whom the Asperger's diagnosis is named, notes that autistic children are often tormented and rejected by their classmates. This happens simply because they are different and stand out from the crowd: "Thus, in the playground or on the way to school one can often see an autistic child at the center of a jeering horde of little urchins. The child himself may be hitting out in blind fury or crying helplessly. In either case he is defenseless."[2]

When I was a student in special education classes in sixth grade, a close friend and classmate was a frequent target of bullying. When teased mercilessly, he often escaped from school and ran faster than a cheetah on performance-enhancing drugs to his home seven miles away. This caused the middle school administration and teachers to panic and call the police department.

In the second grade I experienced terror while riding on the school bus. A fifth-grade bully, who seemed to possess a sonar system to detect weak and injured prey, would climb under his seat behind mine, tightly grab my legs, and pull. This made me feel like a vintage wooden German Santa puppet, with strings to make the hands and legs move. My sensory aversion to touch caused me to scream, kick, and wave my hands as I experienced a meltdown. I would hear the bully and his friends laughing and taunting me the rest of the way.

You can help prevent your child from being a target by teaching him or her not to react to bullying but instead to tell an adult. Since bullies feed on reaction, if your child does not react, the bully will quickly lose interest and search for another victim. Richard Maguire, who has Asperger's, says, "Bullies are inadequate people; they cannot deal with confident people who will not be controlled by them."[3]

Taunts are often based on exaggeration or something completely untrue. An example of exaggeration taunting is a bully calling a boy who stutters "Elmer Fudd" and mocking him by continuously saying, "Have you seen a wabbit wun here?" Untrue taunting is a bully spreading malicious rumors such as, "Jim's only date was with his ugly sister, Amy." These two examples are PG-rated compared to what your child will hear every day in the hallways of a public school. When your child faces taunting, teach him or her to focus on staying calm and keeping emotional response to a minimum.

WARNING SIGNS OF BULLYING

Children with autism are less likely than their peers to report being the target of bullying and teasing because they may not intuitively recognize that the acts of other children are examples of bullying. You need to be proactive and alert to the ten main warning signs of bullying.

1. **A reluctance to attend school**. Your child may begin to tell you different reasons he or she does not want to attend school. The most common excuse is a headache or stomachache. If your child becomes reluctant to attend school, ask

him, "Why don't you want to attend school? Is another student bugging you?"

2. **A change in your child's emotions**. Bullying can cause your child to experience depression, fear, anger, or anxiety. If your typically joyful child is experiencing depression and has withdrawn from peers, ask: "What is causing you to withdraw from your friends? Has anyone at school been saying hurtful words?"

3. **A change in daily routine**. This can include not participating on a team, not attending a youth group, or not participating in routine after-school activities. It can be a change in diet and sleeping patterns or a change in friends. If you notice a change in your child's daily routine, take time to ask what is behind this behavior.

4. **Torn clothing or damaged books and other items**. Bullies will often steal from their victims and damage their belongings. For fear of appearing weak, most children are afraid to tell their parents that a bully has been doing this. One way of gathering information is to talk with your child's friends. Young children will usually tell you exactly what happened. Your son's friend, John, may say, "Jack stole your son's Bulls jacket when he tried to run from him."

5. **Frequent crying spells or expressions of self-doubt**. Perhaps your child goes to his room after school and cries, or you hear him crying at night in his bed. Self-doubt talk means your child calls himself a loser or states, "I feel like everyone hates me."

6. **Feelings of hopelessness or despair**. When this happens, your child, once normally happy, begins to display a cynical or dark view on life.

7. **Expressing no interest in anything**. Adolescents and teenagers frequently change their interests, but having no interest and a general displeasure or apathy toward anything and everything is a sign of bullying or depression.

8. **Cuts or bruises on your child**. Bullies are known for causing physical harm to others. If your child has a black eye or bruises on his body, take the initiative and ask him how he was injured. If a bully does physical harm to your child, report these injuries to the school. Also contact the bully's parents, and if necessary, file a police report.

9. **A decline in academic performance**. Bullying, as mentioned earlier, can affect your child's academic performance.

10. **Increased aggressive behavior**. Bullied children may display violent outbursts and yell or hit children who were not bullying them.

If your child displays any of these warning signs, talk with him about bullying. You can prevent further bullying by providing your child with a counselor, a teacher, or school administrator to whom he can report the abuse and bullying.

Forms of Bullying

The most common form of bullying is verbal aggression, which can include derogatory comments, taunting, name calling, and spreading rumors. Derogatory comments are insulting and disrespectful remarks. For example, "Zack is so horrible at baseball. I could strike him out with my eyes closed." Taunting is mocking or teasing. Bullies often taunt children with autism for their speech impediments or unique repetitive behaviors. They will give their victims derogatory nicknames, such as "retard," "fat," "slut," and "ugly." Bullies often demean children by spreading malicious rumors about them.

Social exclusion and isolation is another form of bullying. Your child may experience bullying by his peers simply not allowing him to participate in fun activities or games. Classmates may perceive your child as awkward due to autism and say, "I don't want Mark on my team. He sucks at kickball."

Your child may be bullied by children stealing his lunch money or damaging his belongings. Another related, clever tactic is a bully harassing your child by manipulating him to do things against his will—possibly even getting him in legal trouble or expelled from school. This type of bullying uses "conditional" friendship. The bully tells an ASD child, "I won't be your friend anymore if you don't steal the cell phone from the store."

Cyberbullying by phone or Internet is also common. Says writer Michael Ko: "The profile of the adolescent bully is changing from the schoolyard thug who extorts fistfuls of lunch money to a more covert operator who avoids face-to-face confrontations in favor of phones and Facebook."[4]

An example of cyberbullying is a bully e-mailing a message to your son, pretending to be a girl he likes and asking him on a date. When he arrives, the bullies are waiting for him.

In *Autism Tomorrow* authors Karen Simmons—founder of the acclaimed AutismToday.com website—and Bill Davis note that cyberbullies will employ e-mails, instant messaging, blogs, chat rooms, or web pages to harass their victims: "They can plot online to attack your child when he arrives at school, spread vicious rumors, set up an embarrassing website, reveal vulnerable information about autism, or send sensitive pictures of your child over the Internet."[5] You can help prevent such malicious tactics by monitoring your child's use of the computer and immediately reporting online abuse to the police.

The most dangerous form of bullying is physical aggression, which can include hitting, kicking, shoving, spitting, or assault with a weapon. Sexually bullying is another ploy. This topic made headlines through the case of two teenage girls in Maryland who sexually assaulted a sixteen-year-old boy with autism and produced a video on their iPhone. If your child is physically or sexually assaulted, you must report the incident to the police department to ensure your child's protection.

METHODS OF BULLY-PROOFING

You can prevent bullies from targeting your child by being proactive. Be alert to the signs of bullying and the different ways bullies harass their victims. Teach your child to understand what bullying is and how to protect himself (or herself) from being bullied. When your child is bullied, discover who the bullies are and contact their parents. Explain to the parents the harmful effects of bullying, that you will not tolerate it, and if another incident should occur, you will report it to the proper authorities. Research the state and county laws on bullying, and familiarize yourself with your child's school policies.

Take a team approach. The team should include parents, the child targeted by bullies, school administration, teachers, a school counselor, and fellow peers. Develop with the team a definition of bullying, and implement an anti-bullying plan. Reflect this plan in your child's Individualized Education Plan (IEP). Insist your child's school adopt a "No Bullying" policy. Lead training seminars on what bullying is, its effects, and how to report it.

Educate students on bullying. Children learn by example. If teachers and staff confront bullying, students are more likely to do the same. Michael John Carley, author of *Asperger's From Inside Out*, wrote, "Students will often emulate the teacher's attitude. And if the teacher is supportive of a student who is different, then the majority of the students will likely follow suit."[6] Use the power of bystanders too—more than 50 percent of bullying situations stop when a peer intervenes. Find a mentor or buddy with whom your child feels comfortable to report any bullying. Mentors can serve as a deterrent to it even happening, since bullies normally prey on a child who is alone.

Teach students and parents autism awareness and acceptance; bullies tend to make fun of children they perceive as "different." So, an understanding of autism can help create acceptance among students. Katie Mecham Celis, whose son has autism, blogged on Facebook:

> Special needs children face being pushed away by kids at school, at church, and in their own neighborhoods. I know from vast experience with these children and with typical children that when parents constantly teach acceptance and love toward those who are different these things happen considerably less. Unfortunately, we live in a society where parents can be just as big of bullies, if not worse by allowing these behaviors to continue.[7]

Teach your child the confidence needed to report bullying to teachers and administrators. This can include enrolling him or her in a self-defense class. By learning to defend themselves, ASD children can be equipped to block kicks and punches and will not be defenseless against bullies.

My Experience

From my elementary through middle school years, I experienced daily bullying from other children. I lived the truth of this observation from Dr. Foster Cline and Jim Fay, coauthors of *Parenting With Love and Logic*: "Generally pre-teens make fun of almost anyone or anything different. All the politically correct 'celebrate diversity' speeches tend to fall on deaf ears in middle school and aren't going to change behavior that may be simply a developmental response at this stage of life."[8]

In the 1980s it was common for children with learning disabilities in the county where I grew up to be transferred annually to another school for a special education program. Between kindergarten and fifth grade I attended four elementary schools. This made it difficult for me to develop lasting friendships and learn vital social skills. I also experienced bullying from older students in my special education classes, since students with learning disabilities were grouped together instead of with others their own age or grade level. In third grade, a fifth grader handcuffed me to the playground equipment and attempted to kidnap Prairie Pup. Luckily the woman overseeing recess foiled his plans and set me free.

In eighth grade, I played on the middle school's track and field, football, and wrestling teams. My dad, a former boxer, taught my brother, Chuck, and me self-defense and boxing techniques. During my first month in middle school, an eighth-grade punk and two of his close friends called me "retarded" and other derogatory names on a daily basis. Whenever these thugs teased me, I would hold my anger inside before hiding in a restroom stall for a private crying session.

Finally, after a month, I had endured enough. When one of my chief tormentors came to my locker and began to tease me, I asked, "If you're so tough and cool, why do you have to call me names?" He took a swing at me, but I blocked his sissy punch with a quick swing of my own and knocked him out! After that I never had a problem with any more of these guys.

In addition to helping me develop new friendships, sports helped stop the bullying. As authors Kathy Labosh and LaNita Miller have observed, participating in sports builds self-confidence, improves motor coordination, and often builds social skills as well.[9] Setting three middle school track-and-field records gained me respect from other students, and I was able to weight lift and train with them. Author Temple Grandin recommends social connections to prevent bullying:

> Until a person participates in activities that are shared with other people, the teasing will continue. I strongly recommend that students with ASD get involved in special interest clubs in some of the areas they naturally excel at, activities such as computers, art, math, karate, etc. These clubs will help provide a refuge from teasing and improve the person's self-esteem. Being with people who share your interests makes socializing easier.[10]

Living the Dream

Doctors diagnosed Anthony Ianni, at the age of four, with pervasive developmental disorder (PDD-NOS). Along with other experts, they warned his parents, "'Don't expect Anthony to be successful in life.' If he graduates from high school—a long shot, at best—he'll probably move into a group home as an adult, where he'll live with others who share his affliction. And athletics? Out of the question. Ianni didn't hear that story until he was in ninth grade, when his father relayed the ominous outlook. By then, Ianni was well on his way to graduating high school and earning a basketball scholarship."[11]

Instead of allowing his autistic traits to be a crutch or hinder him from playing the sport of basketball, Ianni was determined to overcome his disability—and the bullying he

experienced as a youngster. Through hard work and countless hours of practice, he earned a full athletic scholarship to
Grand Valley State University in Allendale, Michigan. Two
years later Ianni transferred to Michigan State University
(MSU) and played for his childhood icon, Coach Tom Izzo.
In 2012 Ianni was part of the Spartans' Big Ten championship
team that made it to the Final Four.

Now a popular motivational speaker, in the fall of 2013
Ianni helped launch the first-ever anti-bullying "Relentless
Tour" for the Autism Alliance of Michigan and the state's civil
rights department. He told me of his struggles with being bullied as a child and says, "As many as 90 percent of children
with autism are targets of bullies. I remember as a child when
a bully tricked me into sticking my tongue on a frozen, metal
pole. Later in life, that same tormenter asked me to autograph
a basketball outside the Breslin Center at MSU. I got the best
out of that bully!"[12]

At six-foot-nine and wearing a size eighteen shoe, Ianni
overshadows all his former tormentors. Basketball was his
path to developing social skills and overcoming adversity. Not
only did it help him silence the bullies, but also his determination made him the first Division I college basketball player
with autism. His message is simple: "Don't give up, and don't
allow others to determine your destiny."[13]

Summary

When you recognize the warning signs and know the different
types of bullying, you can be proactive and help protect your
child. Awareness of bullying and acceptance of others' differences can help parents and students summon the courage to
speak up against bullying. Parents would be wise to remember
that sports and social activities develop self-esteem and relationships, causing your child to cease being a target for bullies.

Chapter 6

REDEFINING YOUR CHILD'S SELF-ESTEEM

I N THE SUMMER I love to swim at our apartment complex's pool or sit nearby reading a book. On one occasion, as I entered the pool area, the lifeguard, Rachel, said, "Please hand me your pool pass!" I handed her my pass and chose a chair in the shade where I could recline. Soft breezes caressed me as I read *Dancing With Max,* the heartwarming story of Emily Colson's (daughter of Prison Fellowship founder Charles Colson) life with her autistic son. Two hours later Rachel announced, "The pool will be closing in ten minutes. Please gather all your belongings." Rachel neatly placed all the yellow pool passes on the check-in table. As I approached, Rachel smiled and pointed to my pass at the edge of the pile as she said, "Your pass is this one unless you want to be someone else!"

Due to their severe disabilities and social struggles, many children with autism indeed wish to be someone else. Your child may dream of being a superhero, star athlete, actor, or just a normal kid. In a joint memoir he coauthored with his mother, *There's a Boy in Here,* Sean Barron commented, "My own worthlessness overwhelmed me. I spent an awful lot of time wishing I were a different person. Why couldn't I be normal?"[1]

I know just how he feels. My self-esteem tank often sat on

empty, thanks to feeling so different. That stemmed from a combination of my unusual routines, unacceptable social behavior, and constant bullying, particularly in middle school. When I failed to make the eighth-grade baseball team, I felt broken and rejected. I wished that I too could have friends like everyone else and be popular.

Like me, many children with autism tend to lag at least six years behind in social and emotional development, which contributes to their low self-image. Therapy, medical examinations, and special education classes also can cause your child to feel different. (Not surprisingly, individuals with autism experience a higher rate of unemployment and underemployment.) Observes Karen L. Simmons, the founder and CEO of Autism Today: "The frequent visits to doctors, or speech therapists, or OTs (occupational therapists), the testing and the stream of interventions that we try with our children can easily leave them feeling like they're under the microscope, a specimen that warrants investigation, a person who needs fixing."[2]

TOTAL RECALL

On 6/18/14 I called the nearby Chevrolet dealer about a recall notice on my 2006 Saturn Ion. After answering the phone, a representative in the service department asked, "What's your eight-digit VIN number?"

"6Z145603," I replied.

Three minutes later, the man said, in a matter-of-fact tone, "Sir, I just want to let you know that your 2006 Saturn is a salvage car."

Just like what happened later on my anniversary trip to Israel, the honey badger sprang from his burrow. Enraged, I blurted, "I bought my Ion new on 11/12/05 from the Saturn dealership in Utica, and it had only thirty-four miles. I paid sticker price, minus my dad's GM employee discount. The dealer even gave me flowers and a Target gift card worth $500 as an incentive as a first-time-buyer."

As the words rushed from my mouth, my neurons flickered erratically, like an electric cord dropped in water. My back tightened and my muscles bulged like Popeye's when he swallows a can of spinach. I was ready for an all-out war.

"Your Saturn title should be branded as a salvage car," he replied. "You purchased your car right after Katrina. The dealer probably scammed you into purchasing a 'New Orleans Special.'"

"As soon as I get off this phone, I will be heading to the dealership like a hurricane!" I replied.

"Wait one minute, sir. Let me recheck your VIN number before you get all bent out of shape and go ballistic."

"6Z145603," I repeated.

"Did you say a three at the end?" he asked. "I put an eight at the end before!"

After a three-minute wait, he returned with an apology.

"No worries; it was the wrong VIN number. Your Saturn is not a salvage car. In two weeks to two months, we should have the parts."

"Thank you," I said, wiping sweat from my face.

Nobody wants to discover the new car they purchased from the dealership has been branded "salvage." Yet many children with autism feel like a salvage car—unwanted and rejected. Society and their peers have placed derogatory labels on them, furthering their feelings of low self-esteem. Among its characteristics are fear of trying new things, negative self-talk, a tendency to be overly critical of self, viewing temporary setbacks as permanent, and a pessimistic attitude toward life.

Parents can help their child develop self-esteem and redefine their self-image by praising their gifts and interpersonal relationships. While anyone can carry this too far and wind up with a self-centered child who thinks he or she is the center of the universe, that isn't too serious a danger with someone whose self-esteem is battered and bruised. As entrepreneur and best-selling author Brian Tracy says, "People with high self-esteem are the most desired and desirable people in society."[3]

Some qualities of healthy self-esteem include knowing one's strengths and weaknesses, feeling good about personal accomplishments, confidence in handling conflicts, assertiveness at school and work, and an ability to resist negative pressures. All are positive—and needed—qualities for ASD children.

After all, a high self-esteem can empower children with stunted development to overcome disabilities and develop social skills. I developed my self-esteem by running on the track team and becoming friends with my peers. My success in track also helped me to succeed in academics and employment. The most effective means to helping your child develop self-esteem is unconditional love and acceptance. Praise your child for his or her gifts and the values he or she brings to your family.

PRECIOUS GIFT

View your child as a precious gift and treasure. Because your child's disabilities may cause him or her to feel isolated and unloved on the playground, the home should be a safe haven where ASD children know they are loved unconditionally. Correct ill-advised behaviors by sandwiching the correction in the middle of positive feedback. For example: "John, you did an awesome job cleaning your room. If you could put your sock by your bed in the hamper, it would look perfect. Thanks so much for all the help you're given us today." Offer tangible rewards and praise too: "For cleaning your room and mowing the lawn, here is money to purchase the video game you want."

Refrain from such negative comments as, "Why can't you be more like your older sister? She listens to us." Or, "Can't you remember to put the toilet seat down?" Refrain from absolute statements too (they often aren't true anyway), such as, "John, you *never* clean your room," or "Why do you *always* forget to do your homework?" Children with autism have difficulty controlling their emotions, and such negative comments can lead to a meltdown.

REGULATING EMOTIONS

Teach your child to regulate his or her emotions by stating feelings as a verb instead of a state of being. Verbs are actions. Our behavior is composed of our daily actions, and we can monitor our behavior through self-awareness. If your child feels sad because his beloved pet lizard died, teach him or her to express those feelings: "I am crying because my lizard died." In this case, the feeling ceases to be an abstract concept. The child can choose to change feelings and bring a healing to otherwise negative expressions of emotions.

Say your daughter is depressed after receiving a poor grade on her English test. Teach her to regulate her emotional feelings by stating, "I am depressing because I studied three hours and still received a D on the test." If your son feels anxious from the sound of tapping pencils in his math class, he can tell the instructor, "I am stressing because of the sound of the tapping pencils. May I please have a time out?" Adding an "ing" to some feeling words is poor English but good behavioral therapy. Feelings stated as verbs can help children with ASD discover they have the power to regulate their emotions and control their actions.

EMOTIONAL AND SENSORY ISSUES

One of the reasons children on the ASD spectrum have problems monitoring and altering their emotions is their emotional arousal can be compared to an on-off electric switch instead of a dial knob that gradually increases and decreases settings. Dr. Valerie L. Gaus, a clinical psychologist who provides mental health services to people with autism, says of one of her clients, "His anger goes from 0 to 60 in a millisecond."[4]

I know how that feels. As a young child, I experienced extreme difficulties managing my emotions. When I became frustrated or angry, I would scream and repeatedly bang my head full-force against the bedroom wall. I also struggled to regulate my sense of fear and anxiety. At the age of five I went with my family to a movie theater for the first time. During one of the previews a hand began to expand; after it covered the whole screen, it suddenly exploded. The unexpected *blam!* caused me to have a meltdown. I screamed, cried, and ran from the theater. My mom had to take me home—immediately. More than thirty-five years later I can still picture that exploding glove.

Sensory issues can cause other children and parents to view your child as different. In third grade, I was attending a Cub Scout event when a goofy, red-nosed clown with a lamb sock puppet grabbed my cap and placed it on another kid's head. The sensation of the clown touching my head and placing my cap on the other child caused a honey badger moment. I quickly yelled, snatched the clown's puppet, and struck him in the head with it. It looked like a scene from a Homey D. Clown skit on the 1990s sitcom *In Living Color*: "I don't think so. Homey don't play that," I said as I imitated Homey's speech and habit of beating someone upside the head with his dirty brown sock.

Teaching your child to understand his or her emotions and regulate fear and anxiety will help build self-esteem. Your child's emotions may fluctuate throughout the day, depending on the level of stimulus. As children learn to adapt to these changes in their emotions, they will have self-confidence to express themselves and try new things.

REDEFINE SELF-IMAGE

Redefine your child's self-image. Self-image is how we perceive ourselves in relationship to others. Thanks to frequent bullying and rejection, most children with autism have a poor self-image. Life experiences cause them to see a warped reflection through muddy water. You can redefine your child's poor self-image by celebrating his gifts and talents and not limiting his potential. As I said earlier, don't focus on the things your child cannot do, but what he is able to do. Praise your child for his uniqueness and differences. Alexis Wineman, a young woman with autism who became Miss Montana in 2012, counsels parents, "Yes, we are different, but why try to fit in when we were made to stand out?"[5]

The story of the lion cub beautifully illustrates the power of redefining self-image. A shepherd in Kenya was leading his sheep to a pasture when he discovered an abandoned lion cub whose mother had been shot by poachers. The shepherd decided to raise the cub with his sheep. The little cub followed the flock and even ate grass like his woolly friends. A few years passed, and the cub was now a mature lion. He still acted like a skittish sheep. Another lion prowled upon the flock, sending the sheep and the lion (who thought he was a sheep) running.

The next day as the lion drank water with the flock, he saw his reflection in the pond and realized he was the "king of the jungle." The lion now knew his true identity and strength (meaning it was pretty *baa, baa, bad* for those sheep). Like that cub, your child has amazing talents waiting to be refined. So praise your child for each step of progress, no matter how small.

Alexis Wineman describes redefining her self-esteem:

> Even after my diagnosis nothing changed, not until I realized that being different isn't something to hide. I came out of the shadows, but very slowly, and for once no one

pushed me back. I stretched my legs and I started to run.
I wanted to make up for all the time I had lost, but I also
did not want to be crushed. I got involved in after school
programs, like cross-country, speech and drama, cheerleading, student council, and so much more! Some of
these efforts were more successful than others, I might
say, but I learned from all of them. I was able to show off
who I was, instead of hiding it like I had in the past.[6]

Praise Progress

Start with small tasks and use them as building blocks. Self-
esteem expands with accomplishments. Success in small projects, like building a tree house, could give your child the
confidence to attend college. Mark Youngkin, the father of
three sons with autism, told me, "Become interested in the
activities and toys your child loves, and invest quality time
with him. Your interest will help your child develop self-
esteem."[7] If your child loves playing with LEGOs, praise him
when he makes a cool LEGOs city. Since many children with
autism are behind in their age development, praise represents
a powerful motivational tool to encourage your child to pre-
serve and overcome disabilities.

Every day my mom would spend time drawing pictures of
animals with me. She would praise me for the detail in my
drawings and encourage me to continue creating art. Her passion in helping me with my pictures caused art class to be my
favorite subject. Drawing gave me great joy, and I felt confidence showing my art projects to peers.

Positive Thinking

Children with disabilities have a tendency to display negative
self-talk and thinking patterns. As a result, your child may
have an all-or-nothing mind-set, be obsessed with certain

thoughts, or take everything personally. An all-or-nothing mind-set uses words like *only, never, must, can't,* and *always.* It views the world in absolutes; things are either all good or all bad. For example, "If I am not first-string on the football team, I will never be good at football." This kind of perfectionism will destroy your child's self-esteem since he or she can never achieve unrealistic expectations.

Teens and young adults with Asperger's can easily become obsessive in relationships. Obsessive thoughts can limit your child from enjoying life and seeing possibilities, which can build self-esteem. If your high school son with Asperger's has an obsession with the beautiful cheerleader, Jane, in his gym class, it causes him to stare at her and not interact with his peers. The football jocks, who notice your son's obsession with Jane, may decide to cyberbully him with a pseudo invitation from Jane to an after-game party. Meanwhile, his obsession with Jane hinders him from talking with Karen, a nice girl in his English class who secretly admires him.

Teaching your child to analyze his thoughts can help him to verbalize obsessive thought patterns and see new opportunities for success. When your child has a new friend, encourage him not to become obsessed with the relationship but allow time for the friendship to blossom. In this way he can continue other friendships and avoid tunnel vision.

Negative thoughts will cause your child to have low self-esteem. Such thoughts as "No one wants to be my friend because I am stupid" or "Everything I do fails; I am not good at anything" set children back. Those with ASD often confuse their feelings or beliefs with fact. For example, they may think, "I feel like a failure, so I must be a failure."

Danger Zone

During the 1997 Super Bowl, Nissan aired a commercial with a flock of pesky pigeons and their general, BB. In a speech to his comrades, General BB declared, "We're going to test your skills and see what you're made of. When you're up there, remember you're not just birds, you're pigeons!" "Danger Zone" played softly in the background as the pigeons took flight over a car wash. Just then General BB announced, "I've spotted a gold mine with a freshly washed beauty."

The army of pigeons quickly descended on the black Nissan, sending torpedo droppings in every direction. The driver skillfully weaved in and out of traffic to avoid dirty bombs on his freshly washed car.

"He's still clean, BB, and almost home free!" Skyrocket declared.

"OK, Skyrocket, I'll get him!" says BB. "I am closing in."

In a last-ditch effort to leave his mark, General BB swooped full-speed downward. The driver's garage door closed, preserving his shining Nissan. After a *thud*, a stunned BB called "Medic!" with his aching beak plastered in the wooden door.

Likewise, your child's mind can become messy and clouded by negative and self-defeating thoughts—what I call "pigeon bombs." You can train your child to take those negative thoughts captive and be proactive in his thought life. The Nissan driver acted proactively by weaving in and out of traffic to avoid the onslaught. While your child cannot prevent birds (negative thoughts) from flying over his home (mind), you can teach him to keep them from building a nest. As my friend, Travis, says, "What you think about, and what you talk about, is what you're about." Teach your child to send away the negative thoughts by choosing to speak positive thoughts.

Remind your child that his thoughts will influence his talk.

Talk will guide behavior, which will impact feelings and emotions. Positive talk will make a huge impact on the development of your child's self-esteem. Since they are so often singled out for bullying or ridicule, it isn't surprising that many ASD children take everything *so personally.* If Mark's friend, John, forgot to call him back, Mark may say, "Mom, John is mad at me. That's why he did not call me the last two nights." In reality, Mark failed to realize John had a test to study for and couldn't find extra time to make a call.

At times I still struggle with taking things personally. I have learned that not only are people often just busy, but also life is full of the unexpected. When people fail to call me back or don't remain faithful to their commitments, there are often extenuating circumstances. Says psychologist Wendy Lawson, who has Asperger's (and a son on the autism spectrum), "Until recently I always believed that if someone close to me was 'angry' then it must be because of me. Now I am beginning to realize that people can be unhappy or even angry, for many different reasons. In fact, it may have nothing to do with me at all."[8]

When you model positive talk for your child, he will follow your example. If you instruct your child to be positive while every word from your mouth is hurtful or negative, your child's speech will match yours. Be mindful of the words you use. Strive to follow the rule of speaking seven positive words for every critical one. Speak blessings and life over your child. And remember that positive talk attracts healthy relationships. People love to hear inspiring and encouraging words.

As part of your pattern of positive talk, teach your child to forgive his or her mistakes. Teach them that mistakes are a part of life, not a permanent reflection on them as a person. When your child makes a mistake, teach them to declare, "I made a mistake, but that mistake doesn't define me as failure." Forgiveness silences self-doubt talk.

Positive Relationships

Positive relationships will help your child feel valued and loved. I experienced difficulty developing and maintaining positive relationships. When I met new people, I would often bore them with my special interest topics or attempts to dominate the conversation. My mom and dad taught me the importance of listening and taking an interest in other people. Three main ways you can help your child develop strong interpersonal relationships are teaching him or her to be an active listener, to share, and to demonstrate a willingness to participate in social activities.

Teach your child to be an active listener.

Children with autism tend to fail at social graces and misinterpret communication clues. Autism can cause your child to be excessively focused on his or her interests and miss the yawn of the bored listener. Teach your child to be an active listener by asking reflective questions. "What made your day good?" Make a list of questions to ask when meeting someone new, such as, "What are some of the things you like to do for fun?" Role-play social situations your child will encounter, and teach the proper responses. Providing a mentor is the best method of helping your child learn social graces.

Teach your child the art of sharing.

Children with autism have difficulty sharing because it breaks their rigid routines and patterns. Sharing also requires empathy. You can teach your child to share by playing board games that require taking turns and peer interaction. When your child shares with other children, reward that good behavior with praise.

Help your child to join social activities related to his special interests.

Sensory issues can cause social activities to be quite a challenge. Nurturing your child's strengths and gifts will also build his social skills and self-esteem. Children will take an interest in your child's gifts and want to learn from him or her. My brother, Chuck, and I were friends a boy whose autism made him a savant at video games. When we invited him to sleepovers, our friends would stay up all night, watching with amazement as he won both Castlevania and Super Mario Bros. games.

ACCEPTANCE

Children with high self-esteem accept the things they can't change. As a parent, you may be challenged with acceptance of your child's progress at annual Individualized Education Planning (IEP) meetings. You may feel discouraged to learn that your son, Mark, is five years behind in his age group in average reading comprehension. Don't tell Mark, "You're way behind the other kids. If you don't practice reading with me every night, you'll never catch up." Instead, encourage Mark by saying "I see all the hard work you put into reading. Let's spend a little more time to increase your talent."

For adults with Asperger's, one of the toughest challenges of self-acceptance is annual employment evaluations. Having the boss sit in front of them while evaluating strengths and weaknesses can prompt feelings of fear and anxiety. During such sessions I shared with my boss my strengths and explained my blind spots that stem from autism. I would end my evaluations by stating, "I am not different. I think normally for an individual with Asperger's. My mind processes information more literally and in picture form. Everyone has strengths and weaknesses due to his or her neurological processing."

"I will admit, personal acceptance is a roller coaster," says former Miss Montana Alexis Wineman. "Despite the strides I have made, I still struggle with some things, and I am finding new challenges as I enter adulthood. No matter how tough it gets, I know that the scared, hopeless, young girl I once was is now a more confident young woman who is no longer ashamed."9

Acceptance phrases build self-esteem. Some of my acceptance phrases are:

- I accept that my brain processes information differently from that of others.

- I accept that unexpected things happen in life and I may have to adjust my routines to accommodate them.

- I accept that I experience anxiety and fear, but I will not let those feelings hold me back.

- I accept that I sometimes feel overwhelmed by sensory overload. When this happens, I will take a break.

- I accept that my being different does not make me inferior to others.

- Autism does not define me. I define autism.

- I am fearfully and wonderfully made.

- I will never give up on myself.

- I accept myself for who I am.

NOTHING IS IMPOSSIBLE

The story of Alexis Wineman beautifully illustrates the power of redefining your child's self-image. Kim Wineman and her husband, Michael, quickly noticed a neurological difference between Alexis and her twin sister, Amanda. When Alexis grew frustrated or cried, her whole body would tighten up for hours. Nothing seemed to bring Alexis relief from her meltdowns.

Alexis was delayed in her motor skills while Amanda reached developmental milestones on time. Alexis demonstrated difficulties walking and speaking, but the whole family babied her. Their neighbors reasoned: "Alexis is fine. She's behind in development because she's the baby of the family."

At school Alexis's heavy speech impediment led to verbal abuse. Children called Alexis "a retard" and told her she was not worth the breaths she drew. Eventually Alexis stopped talking to avoid attention. Then, in the fourth and fifth grades, she began displaying behavioral problems. Kim felt devastated when Alexis's teacher referred to her adorable daughter as "the pokey little puppy." Math equations took Alexis twice as much time to solve. When she became angry and frustrated from struggles with algebra, the instructor would send her to the hallway to calm down.

After school Alexis would withdraw for hours to her room and shut down from interaction with her family. When upset, she would bang her head relentlessly against the wall or descend into a screaming tantrum. Desperate for help, her parents sought counsel from their pastor. He wisely advised: "Alexis's behavioral issues require professional help. She needs to be evaluated by a therapist."

After intensive neurological testing, doctors diagnosed Alexis (by now eleven) with pervasive developmental disorder (PDD-NOS) and borderline Asperger's. A psychiatrist prescribed an antidepressant, which had terrible side effects, causing Alexis to become more withdrawn and depressed. "Nobody understood what I was going through," she says. "I separated myself from my classmates and spent most of my time alone. I stayed quiet to hide my speech problems. Due to these overwhelming and daily struggles, I looked at myself as a punching bag for others, and a burden to my family."[10]

Still, Kim was determined to help her daughter overcome autism by developing her self-esteem. Kim encouraged Alexis to use her talent of drawing. Alexis learned social skills as she competed on the cross-country team, cheerleading squad, and drama group. Kim jokes, "I was the Cut Bank High School cheerleader coach. So I forced Alexis to join our team."[11] Today, Kim encourages parents of children with special needs, "Find your child's niche that involves other people."[12]

As an example of this kind of socialization, Alexis loved playing PlayStation games, but typically did so by herself. The drama group, composed of students considered by their peers as "misfits," encouraged Alexis to leave her comfort zone and perform comedy routines. While competing for Miss Montana and Miss America, Alexis used the skills she developed— thanks to the group's encouragement—to win over the audience. Likewise, Kim instructs parents: "Teach your child to leave her comfort zone and learn new things. This will develop her confidence to handle real-life situations."[13]

As Alexis entered her senior year of high school, she asked her mom, "What scholarships are available for college?" Kim provided her daughter with a list that included the Miss Montana program. A few days later Alexis excitedly told her parents, "I am going to compete for Miss Montana." Kim's and Michael's jaws hit the carpet in terror. "*Miss Montana?*" they thought. "Alexis doesn't like makeup or the sensation of fancy clothes."

Despite her parents' misgivings, Alexis was determined. However, on the first night of competition, Alexis felt overwhelmed. Though confident on the stage, she experienced social awkwardness among fellow contestants. After three days of competition, though, Alexis and her family were amazed as she was crowned Miss Montana. In January of 2013, on *World News Tonight*, ABC News anchor Diane Sawyer named Alexis her "Person of the Week."

Alexis's platform for Miss America in 2012 was titled, "Normal Is Just a Dryer Setting: Living With Autism." While competing for Miss America, Alexis advocated for autism by wearing a light blue evening gown to match the color of the puzzle piece symbol of Autism Speaks. A few hours into the pageant, Alexis exclaimed to a fellow contestant with tears, "Holy crap, I'm in Miss America!" Alexis's message is, "Autism doesn't define me. I define it." She was voted "America's Choice," earning her a spot in the live show competition with the other top sixteen contestants.

Alexis often shares at autism conferences: "I will be successful if just one person encounters a child who is overstimulated without staring. If one teenager invites an 'outcast' to lunch or just smiles at him or her. Or if one employer gives a job to someone who might not be able to look the interviewer in the eye."[14]

Alexis's goal is to use her unique opportunities to be a voice for those who don't have one and redefine peoples' perspectives of autism. "Being on the autism spectrum is not a death sentence but a life adventure," she says. "We need to understand autism and help those with the condition to unlock the potential that lies within all of us."[15]

SUMMARY

One of the best gifts you can give your ASD child is self-esteem. You can help your child develop self-esteem by redefining his self-image through praise, helping him learn to manage emotions, and teaching your child about positive thoughts and speech, healthy relationships, and acceptance. Self-esteem will empower your child to be confident in social settings and feel the freedom to use his or her talents.

Chapter 7

THE POWER OF ADVOCACY

A N "ADVOCATE" STANDS up to plead the cause of another. Advocacy means standing up for your ASD child's rights and helping him or her to receive public accommodations. It is a lifelong commitment to empower your child to receive the resources that can help lead to his or her independence and success. The weakest voice deserves the greatest defense. In biblical terms, this includes defending the helpless, using every available resource, using tenacity and boldness, and placing your child's cause into God's hands. (For a detailed examination, see "Biblical Principles of Advocacy" in appendix C.)

Advocacy can be as simple as requesting extended time from your child's teacher for a math test or as complicated as a filing a major Americans With Disabilities Act (ADA) civil rights case—which is what my parents did in *Sandison v. MHSAA*.

As a parent, some of the main areas you will need to advocate for your child concern school services with your child's Individualized Education Plan (IEP), therapy, employment, and additional government-funded resources available from the county or state. In college I needed a computer to accommodate my learning disabilities. After my mom championed my cause with Michigan Rehabilitations Services (MRS), I received a check for $1,500 to use to purchase a new computer.

My mom also served as an advocate for help with my

college tuition. As a result, I received $2,500 a year from MRS to help pay for my undergraduate studies. Advocating requires networking with other parents of special-needs children and researching information regarding possible government grants for special services. One parent whose son has a learning disability encouraged my mom to make use of MRS' resources. Today, my mother advises other parents of special-needs children: "Advocate, advocate, advocate, and when your child is mature, he or she will be an advocator."

One of the greatest skills I learned from my mom is the ability to be an advocate for my rights. In this chapter I will share effective methods for acting as your child's advocate. Through your advocacy, your child will learn to advocate for himself or herself.

PLEADING MY CAUSE

While writing this book, I had to use my advanced advocacy skills. Ten minutes before my phone interview with Dr. Norman Woeller—one of the leading medical experts on autism—I paced back and forth in my apartment, clutching my cell phone as I nervously awaited the time to place the call. (I had scheduled this interview a month in advance.) Suddenly I heard a deafening grinding sound coming from a board sliding outside my apartment. It sounded like the snapping of huge, two-by-four-sized toothpicks. Opening my door, I saw two maintenance men with crowbars.

"I have sensory issues due to autism, and I need you to quit working outside my apartment for an hour," I told them in a gentle but firm tone. "I have a phone interview with an internationally known expert on autism for my book."

They laughed. The taller one said, "I have a work order to put new siding around these doors. So I won't stop until I am done. You can call my boss—good luck!"

"Can I have your boss's number?"

"I can't give you his number. Like I said, good luck!"

I quickly called the apartment office and explained my need for the maintenance men to postpone their work until I finished my interview. The staff member told me I needed to talk with a more senior representative and gave me the number for the person I should call.

My hands shook as I dialed.

"How may I help you?" a female voice answered.

I proceeded to inform her of my dilemma, explaining my sensory issues from autism and need for accommodation, stating, "I should've been notified two weeks in advance about the renovations. Then I would've made other arrangements for my interview."

"Those two maintenance men are paid by the hour. I'll not have them cease from their work for an hour while you interview the expert on autism—even if you have sensory issues," she replied. "My boss does not make money by having his employees work for free."

"Ignorance of the Americans With Disabilities laws does not grant you noncompliance to ADA federal requirements for accommodations for a disability," I said. "Your company's ignorance is not a safeguard from any legal actions for your choosing not to comply with the ADA standards. Google my name on your iPhone, and you'll see *Sandison v. MHSAA*. If you don't comply with the ADA requirements, the next time you google my name, you'll see it next to your company's name in another lawsuit ruling."

Two minutes later the lead maintenance guy said, "I don't know what you said. Our boss just called and told us to get out of here immediately."

"Before we have a major lawsuit!" exclaimed the second maintenance worker.

The power of advocacy gained me a new respect with those workers and allowed my interview to proceed as scheduled.

DISCLOSURE CONSIDERATIONS

Advocacy involves disclosing your child's autism diagnosis. Says Jesse Saperstein, the author of *Getting a Life With Asperger's*: "Disclosure is the fragile artistry of revealing that you have a sometimes difficult, often beautiful condition and how to best educate the public. When do you disclose and whom do you want to tell? And when is it best to just remain silent?"[1]

So, when should you disclose your child's autism? If your child understands his ASD diagnosis, ask your child if he wants you to disclose this information. Some questions to consider before revealing this information include:

- Who needs to know, and why?
- What are the benefits, or possible negative consequences, of disclosure?
- Could disclosure lead to your child facing discrimination or suffering attacks on his or her self-esteem?

However, recognize that disclosure is important to establish evidence of disability in order to receive accommodations and necessary resources. It may have other positives, which professional surfer Clay Marzo discovered.

A SURFBOARD FREAK

One of the world's most creative surfers, Marzo is known for his "double-jointed" style of turns and spins. Mitch Varnes, a former editor of *Surfing* magazine and now principal of Board

Sports Management (which represents Clay), says this prodigy is so innovative it defies traditional surfing terms, leaving people grasping for words to describe his moves. Nine-time world surfing champion Kelly Slater marvels at his ability. "Clay is a freak on a surfboard," he says. "He does things people don't even think of. He has his own way of seeing the waves."[2]

While his professional peers are amazed at his unique skills, in the past many were also baffled by his quirks and odd behavior. Disclosing his diagnosis of Asperger's helped his fans and sponsors to better understand his social awkwardness and aloofness. I learned more about this situation through a telephone interview with his mother, Jill.

Thanks to her motherly instincts, she sensed early in life that Clay was unique and different from his older brother, Shane. When Jill nursed Clay, he would twirl her hair. Then at seven months of age Clay abruptly quit nursing without any weaning. As a four-year-old, Clay would line seashells in a ridge pattern along the beach. But when Jill told a five-year-old Clay, "Please tie your shoes," he replied in a soft tone, "Mommy, I don't understand what you're saying."[3]

Asperger's caused Clay to be gifted on water but struggle on land with communication and social skills. His mother told me how Clay once got into a "fender bender" while out driving with his girlfriend. Terrified, he ran from the accident scene and hid in the woods. Clay's girlfriend had to explain to the people in the other car that Clay had autism. He also struggles to finish even a short interview with a reporter, remaining tense and seldom making eye contact. When Clay's routine is altered, keeping him from the ocean, he becomes easily agitated. When Clay is anxious, he flaps his arms; when excited, he repeatedly rubs his hands together.

Problems, yes, but his Asperger's is also his strongest gift. It has given him the ability to zero in on the waves and follow a daily routine of eight-hour surfing sessions—with no breaks. Each day Clay invests another eight hours watching videos of his surfing, endlessly replaying each wave. These sessions have empowered Clay to refine his surfing techniques. Combined with his daily practice, he has learned to maneuver his six-foot-one, 175-pound body gracefully. Marzo declares, "Waves are toys from God."[4] His mother told me, "On dry land, Clay is like a fish out of water, but in the ocean, it's like he can breathe. He has an obsession with water."[5]

Clay was born with this deep connection to water. He swam at just one month, six months before taking his first step on dry land. He had his first boogie board by age two and began to ride four-foot waves on his stomach. He won a state swimming title at ten. At eleven, he signed a professional contract with the legendary Quicksilver team. At age fifteen, he won the men's open division at the National Scholastic Surfing Association championship. Strider Wasilewski, Quicksilver team manager, boasts, "Clay has catlike ability to stay up on his board, bending and contorting his body into seemingly impossible positions, and he is not shy about taking huge risks, often with disastrous results. I knew when I first saw a video of Clay that he would change the face of surfing."[6]

CHALLENGING WAVES

Facing academic difficulties because of learning disabilities, Clay dropped out of high school during his junior year. His teachers thought that he had a "bad attitude" and "lacked motivation," which they incorrectly concluded caused his behavioral issues. One teacher shared that Clay seemed high on dope in class as he often stared off into space and kept to himself. In his earlier days Clay was unable to connect with his fans and openly disliked sponsor and fan gatherings, so much that his career was suffering.

So in 2007 Quicksilver decided to produce a documentary on Clay, titled *Misunderstood*. Jamie Tierney, who was assigned to direct the film during the process of producing the video, noticed that Clay had many characteristics of autism. He contacted Clay's mother and asked if she would agree to have Clay diagnosed. After two months Jill finally agreed. In December 2007 Clay was diagnosed with Asperger's; Jamie revised the title to *Just Add Water*.

After the revelation of his condition, Clay received guidance in developing social skills from other professional sufferers. He also volunteers with Surfers Healers, a nonprofit organization based in Malibu, California. It exposes ASD children to surfing through camps in the United States and Canada. Autism has been a gift that has empowered Clay to be one of the greatest surfers ever and to change his profession.

DISCRIMINATION DRAWBACKS

While it aided Marzo's career, disclosure can create a negative effect if it leads to discrimination. My father experienced the effects of discrimination long ago. In 1961 he graduated from a private technological university with an architectural and engineering degree. During the commencement celebration, my dad said to his friend, Johnny—an African American in his graduating class—"With our degrees in engineering, we will be able to have meaningful and high-paying jobs!"

"That's easy for you to say since you are white," Johnny replied. "But it will be difficult for me to find a job in our field."

My dad always remembered this conversation and taught my brothers and me never to judge others based on religion, race, gender, or disabilities, since everyone is equal in God's sight. Before the civil rights movement in the 1960s, many African Americans experienced racial discrimination and as a result were unemployed or underemployed. Today, many individuals with ASD face similar discrimination in the workplace. As a result, they experience difficulties finding and maintaining employment.

I knew a guy who worked at an agency rehabilitating juvenile offenders. He had been diagnosed with Asperger's in childhood, and though he had a master's degree in social work, he once commented to me, "People like me are the last to be hired and the first to be fired. I just lack the social skills to read people and the social graces to say things that don't offend. I have been fired from my share of jobs the past few years by saying the wrong thing to the wrong person at the wrong time! The only job I am able to maintain is a taxicab driver."

This man lasted only a few months at this agency because of his inability to maintain control over his small group of teens. One time a fourteen-year-old kicked a soccer ball and hit him squarely in the head. About thirty seconds later he responded, "Ah, was I just hit in the head with a soccer ball or something?" as the group roared with laughter. Teens there received rewards of pop and candy, based on receiving a certain number of points in their behavioral program. Not realizing this, this unfortunate man would open the stash containing the children's rewards and say, "Ah, free food for everyone today! No points checking," as he ate a KIT KAT. When confronted by a coworker, he replied, "Rookie mistake!" The last I heard, he was indeed driving a taxicab for a living.

Jesse Saperstein, whom I quoted earlier, wrote in his memoir:

> In the adult world, bullying may re-manifest itself as a wolf in sheep's clothing through unfair job terminations, gingerly worded rejection letters, water cooler gossip, and party snubs. Furthermore, the consequences of adult bullying may extend to chronic unemployment, homelessness and even suicide.[7]

ACCOMMODATIONS

Many individuals with ASD struggle in the workplace and may feel discriminated against due to their inability to cope with stress or relate well to coworkers and clients. Yet the ADA legislation protects individuals with disabilities. Individuals with autism should encourage their employers to offer reasonable accommodations for disabilities, as the act requires. If an employer fails to comply with these standards, they should report this to the US Department of Justice and also to state authorities. (See appendix B, "Reporting an ADA Complaint.")

Melanie Jordan, a training and technical assistance associate at the Institute for Community Inclusion at the University of Massachusetts, outlines the meaning of accommodations and "undue hardship" to employers under the ADA requirements:

> An accommodation is any change in the work environment (or in the way things are usually done). The process applies to all facets of employment, from hiring to orientation and training to workplace events and activities. The purpose is to help a qualified individual with a disability apply for a job, perform the duties of a job and enjoy the benefits and privileges of employment. Accommodations can include modification of work schedule or policy; physical changes to workspace; equipment and devices; job restructuring; adjustment of supervisory methods; and job coaching.
>
> The employment aspects of the Americans with Disabilities Act (ADA, Title I) state that employers are required to make reasonable accommodations for an employee with a disability, as long as the accommodation does not pose an "undue hardship" to the employer. Factors considered under hardship include:
> - the nature and cost of the accommodation.
> - the resources and size of the business.

- the type of business—composition, functions, workforce structure.
- the impact the accommodation would have on the facility and business as a whole.[8]

I know of a woman who has an anxiety disability. The hospital where she works has accommodated her by not mandating her to work in the children's or acute units. The hospital where I work also accommodates me; due to my disability and sensory issues, I am exempt from working the aggressive male and acute units. This has prompted my coworkers to joke, "Ron is not strong enough for the psychotic, aggressive male unit; too childish for the kids unit; and would cause the patients to be more manic and hyper-verbal on the acute unit. So he works just fine in the high-functioning adult unit."

All kidding aside, individuals with ASD have many positive qualities to offer employers. Among them are dependability, a strong work ethic, creativity, and skills with systemizing and memorization. Under ADA law, employers must accommodate people with sensory and social-skills issues and must not allow these disabilities to prevent individuals with ASD from obtaining gainful employment. However, an individual needs to make a request in writing to an employer to receive these accommodations.

Even these provisions don't necessarily make for a smooth employment process for ASD workers. As John Elder Robison, author of *Look Me in the Eye: My Life With Asperger's*, wrote:

> My conversational difficulties highlight a problem Aspergians experience every day. A person with an obvious disability—for example, someone in wheelchair—is treated compassionately because his handicap is obvious.
>
> No one turns to a guy in a wheelchair and yells,

"Quick! Let's run across the street!" And when he can't run across the street, no one says, "What's his problem?" They offer to help him across the street.

With me, though, there is no external sign that I am conversationally handicapped. So folks hear some conversational misstep and say, "What an arrogant jerk!" I look forward to the day when my handicap will afford me the same respect accorded to a guy in a wheelchair. And if the respect comes with a preferred parking space, I won't turn it down.[9]

CREATING AN IEP

Parents have a responsibility to help their children with ASD learn basic skills that will empower them to function within society and be employable as adults. Some of these essential skills are proper hygiene, healthy self-esteem, dependability, diplomacy, polite manners, self-advocating, and workplace politics. In your child's Individualized Education Plan (IEP), have these essential qualities listed for him or her as learning goals.

Under federal law, school districts must provide special education services for children from ages three to twenty-one. The IEP grew out of other past legislation, starting with the Education of Handicapped Children Act of 1974. This bill was signed into law the following year and would be followed by the Individuals with Disabilities Education Act (IDEA) of 1997. This legislation established IEPs to address each child's unique learning issues and include specific educational goals.

For your child to have an IEP, the school must determine whether your child qualifies for special education services. To qualify, your child's disability must have an adverse effect on his or her educational progress and hinder the child's ability to learn. Just having a disability does not automatically establish eligibility. The school will ask you to provide documented proof of your child's disabilities in the form of evaluations and reports from doctors and/or therapists.

An IEP is a combination contract—it is a both a legal document and a guide for a child's education. The IDEA law requires your child's IEP to be created based on the child's needs, not the district's preexisting programs or other services. The plan describes in detail the services your child is to receive, modifications and accommodations, the educational goals, and the curriculum for your child's schooling. Federal law also requires that every IEP contain annual education goals. For these goals to be effective, they need to be specific, realistic, and measurable. This is vital—it's how you and the team can tell if your child is progressing.

"Mark will develop writing skills" is not a specific or measurable goal, since that will make it tough to monitor his improvement. An example of a specific, realistic, and measurable goal is, "Given a fourth-grade book, Mark will be able to read a passage orally at ninety to one hundred words per minute with fewer than ten errors."

The IEP team develops the goals in the IEP meeting at the beginning of each school year. When evaluating your child's goals, discuss your child's progress toward his goals and how often you will be informed of his or her progress. Standardized tests and curriculum-based measurements (CBM) are two effective methods of measurement. CBM involves teachers performing brief tests to evaluate your child's progress. When IEP goals are written in a specific and measurable manner, this information can provide you with an accurate evaluation of your child's progress. Make sure the IEP team agrees in writing to inform you with each report card of your child's progress toward these goals.

IEP's ACCOMMODATIONS

Some services you may request in your child's IEP for accommodation can include specially designed instruction, supplementary aids, program modifications, related services, classroom accommodations, and a resource room.

Specially designed instruction means adapting the content or delivery of the curriculum to address your child's unique educational needs based on his strengths and weaknesses. Supplementary aids can provide additional classroom support for your child. Program modifications may include lowered success criteria for academic qualifications, decreased alternative state assessments, and a change in the content of the program to meet your child's unique needs.

Related services are additional accommodations your child needs and can include such things as speech therapy, occupational or physical therapy, interpreters, medical services, counseling, and transportation. My mom successfully advocated that the school provide additional tutoring for me in math and English.

Classroom accommodations include such provisions as extended time for assignments and tests, using oral tests and quizzes in place of written ones, taking tests in a separate (quiet) room, use of a laptop, copies of the teachers' notes, and others. When I took Greek at ORU, the school always provided me with extended test time.

A resource room is a separate, remedial classroom in a school where your child can receive individual assistance with tests and assignments. Your child's IEP should contain any accommodations required for him or her to progress toward stated goals.

IEP's Advocacy

You may not agree with the school's recommendations about your child's IEP and education. Under the law, you have the right to challenge decisions concerning your child's eligibility, evaluation, placement, and the services the school offers. If you disagree with the school's actions or refusal to take action in these matters, you have several options:

Try to reach an agreement with the school. You can meet with school administrators to discuss your concerns and attempt to reach an agreement. You can try a temporary solution; for example, agree to evaluate your child's placement for a certain period of time and see how he or she does. This offers a win-win for you and the school.

Ask for mediation. During mediation, you and the school meet with someone who is not involved in the disagreement and try to reach an agreement.

Ask for due process. In a due process hearing, you and the school personnel appear before an impartial hearing officer and present your issues and concerns. The hearing officer decides how to solve the problem.

File a complaint with the state education agency. To file a complaint, you usually have to write directly to the State Education Agency and cite the section of the IDEA law you feel the school has violated. The agency has sixty calendar days to resolve your complaint.

Become familiar with laws established to help those with disabilities, especially those dealing with special education. Familiarity with laws will help you know the services your child is entitled to receive. Nobody is likely to offer them unless you request them, and you may have to be your child's advocate to obtain them.

Contact your local media, and if necessary, find an attorney. When you have exhausted all your resources and followed the steps outlined above, and the school still refuses the accommodations your child needs, contact local media. Find an attorney who specializes in disability rights and special education issues. As I mentioned earlier, my senior year, the school refused to let me compete on the track and cross-country teams due to my being past the eligibility age. My mom advocated for me by obtaining an attorney to take my case pro bono. By winning, I was able to receive a college scholarship in track and cross-country.

Summary

Advocacy requires that you use your resources to protect your child's rights and receive the accommodations he or she needs. As you advocate for your child, you will teach him or her to be an advocate. You should use discernment and discretion in determining when and with whom to disclose your child's autism diagnosis. Ask yourself, "Does he or she need to know, and why?" Finally, make sure your child's IEP is realistic, specific, and measurable to meet the goals you intend to achieve. As you advocate for your child's rights, you will empower him or her to be successful.

Chapter 8

ABA THERAPY

A FIVE-YEAR-OLD WITH AUTISM, Jonathan communicated mainly through barely understandable grunts and temper tantrums. His parents, Jim and Jackie, were emotionally and physically drained from driving three hours round-trip three days a week so Jonathan could receive one-on-one applied behavior analysis (ABA) therapy. Jim's insurance plan from the small company where he worked only covered three therapy sessions a week, with a co-pay for the treatments that cost the couple more than $800 a month. The financial strain forced Jackie, a stay-at-home mom, to take a part-time job.

Jonathan's ABA therapist, Krystal, patiently worked to help improve his communication skills. Yet as weeks dragged into months, Jonathan showed little progress. When Krystal pointed at a picture of a cat, Jonathan grunted, "Kor." Still, he showed signs of life. Jonathan loved to spin in circles and flap his hands, and for Krystal to push him on the swings. As she pulled back the seat, Krystal repeatedly said in motherly tones, "Push! Jonathan say, 'Push! Push!' Say, 'Push!'"

Laughing, Jonathan would grunt, "Ush! Ush!"

More months passed, with Jonathan showing only minimal improvement. Krystal continued to faithfully apply the ABA methods tailored for his treatment. Finally, after eighteen months, Jonathan began to say, "Push!" to go higher on the swings. When Krystal smiled and placed a picture of a cat before Jonathan, he laughed and said, "Cat." Jonathan ceased constantly flapping his hands and spinning in circles. When Krystal addressed Jonathan, he would look her in the eyes and smile.

This story illustrates the patience, persistence, and faith needed to guide your child through the therapy process. As you can see, in Jonathan's case therapy was a slow, steady process, but it accomplished miraculous behavioral, communicational, and social transformation. In ABA, therapists teach specific skills by breaking them into smaller steps, teaching each step one at a time and building on the previous one. This process is known as chaining.

Thus, the therapist and family are able to monitor and measure daily progress. Some of the methods used to help the child learn specific skills include prompting (guiding the child by desired response), shaping, and rewarding for correct responses.

After less than two years of ABA therapy, Jonathan had regained most of his communication skills and stopped his repetitive behavior. After seven years Jonathan entered mainstream education, with only an hour a day of special education class.

In this chapter I will examine why ABA therapy is the method accepted by professionals; it owes part of its reputation to Catherine Maurice's popular 1993 book, *Let Me Hear Your Voice: A Family's Triumph Over Autism*. Unlike some other therapies for autism, ABA has scientific research and data demonstrating its results. Because insurance companies are able to review the child's progress based on the recorded data and examine the goals set by the therapists and family, it is one of the few methods they will cover.

In addition, I will review the steps of ABA therapy and how they are practically applied at home and in the community.

Some of the terms in this chapter may seem difficult or confusing, but as you read, I will explain them through stories and examples.

A Basic History of ABA

ABA is the common term for the scientific method of behavior modification. B. F. Skinner is considered its grandfather, due to his groundbreaking research and development of "operant conditioning," explained in his 1938 book, *The Behavior of Organism*. Operant conditioning is a type of learning in which an individual's behavior is sensitive to, and modified by, its consequences. ABA is a process of systematically applying intervention to improve socially significant behaviors.

ABA therapy is based on the philosophy that influencing a response associated with a certain behavior can shape and control that behavior. It is a mixture of psychology and educational techniques, formulated to the needs of each child to help transform his or her behavioral patterns. It includes the use of behavioral methods for measuring behavior, teaching functional skills, and evaluating progress. In one sentence, ABA can be summed up as a continual process of reinforcing responses to desired behaviors with rewards and praise while ignoring, correcting, or redirecting the inappropriate behaviors until the desired behaviors become the norm, and the undesired behaviors fade.

ABA is based on the theory that learned behaviors have an antecedent (something that happened prior to the behavior manifesting itself) and a consequence (what happens as result of the behavior), and that our behavior is formulated by the consequences of our actions. Humans are motivated to repeat behaviors based on the positive or negative consequences they produce. For example, Tom will study twelve hours for his biology test if he expects his studying to be rewarded with a higher exam grade.

If the teacher gave everyone an A-plus just for showing up for the test, do you think Tom would have any motivation to study?

The concept of consequences and rewards in ABA is biblically based. As Hebrews says, "And without faith it is impossible to please God, because anyone who comes to him must believe that he exists and that *he rewards those who earnestly seek him*" (Heb. 11:6, emphasis added). Likewise, in Old Testament times, God promised rewards for keeping His law: "The LORD will make you the head, not the tail. If you pay attention to the commands of the LORD your God that I give you this day and carefully follow them, you will always be at the top, never at the bottom" (Deut. 28:13).

UNDERLYING MEDICAL CONDITIONS

Before beginning any mode of therapy for autism, have your child tested for any underlying medical problems, which can hinder the progress of treatment and learning. Often when an underlying medical problem is addressed and treated, it will lessen the negative effects of autism and maximize therapy improvements.

Says Dr. Kurt Norman Woeller, a biomedical autism specialist:

> Our body is basically a walking chemistry set. When there is an imbalance in [this] chemistry, things start to go wrong. Consider a swimming pool that may have "hard" water (too many minerals) and not enough chlorine—the pool can quickly look like a green swamp! It's the same with your child's body chemistry. The toxins and imbalanced chemistry lead to health and neurological problems. However, when the chemistry is corrected, your child is in a better position for improvement and potential recovery.[1]

Ten Steps of ABA

ABA can be broken into ten main components:

1. Identify the target behavior.

What is the behavior you hope to change? Let's say your son, Mark, acts aggressively toward his sister, Mary. How does Mark display aggressive behavior? By biting Mary's arm. The target behavior you want to change through ABA is getting Mark to stop biting Mary.

2. Discover the baseline of the target behavior under normal circumstances.

Baseline is the frequency and duration of the behavior under normal situations. How often does Mark bite Mary—three times a day or once a week? By answering this question, you will be able to monitor and measure Mark's daily progress. You can gather this data by keeping a chart (event sampling) and counting the frequency of the target behavior of Mark's biting and the length of time of each bite.

Longtime psychologist and behavior analyst Dr. Bobby Newman points out:

> If you don't know the baseline, you will never be truly sure that the behavior is improved and that your intervention was responsible. Without making sure to collect data, we might have over- or under-estimated how much the behavior was actually occurring. It also might have actually been improving already, and your intervention was not responsible for the noted improvement.[2]

3. Identify the antecedents.

What causes Mark to bite Mary? Is there anything that normally happens before his target behavior? Does Mark give a warning sign, such as pacing or yelling first? Does Mark cover his face? The latency of the target behavior can help you iden-tify the antecedent. Latency is the length of time that occurs between the antecedent and behavior. If Mark paces five min-utes in the living room before biting Mary, the latency is the five-minute time frame, and the antecedent is pacing before biting. Figuring out the antecedent of the behavior is often more difficult to discover than the latency.

4. Record the location.

Where does the target behavior usually occur? Does Mark typically bite Mary at home or school? Is Mary using the vacuum in the living room, which triggers Mark's pacing and biting? Or maybe Mark bites Mary because she teases him at school. Leave no stone unturned in uncovering causes.

5. Record the time the behavior normally occurs.

Time can help discern the routine events that occur before the target behavior. Does Mark bite Mary right before lunch-time because he is hungry? Is Mark on medication that wears off near the time of the target behavior?

6. Determine the consequences.

What happens after the target behavior of Mark biting Mary? Often this is more important than the antecedent because the consequences can reinforce the target behavior or cause it to become extinct. When Mark bites Mary, does the teacher gives him attention by lecturing him? If so, this may reinforce the negative behavior. Maybe Mark thinks his teacher looks funny yelling and getting a red face, so Mark continues. By contrast, the teacher could decide to reward Mark with praise for not biting Mary, which would encourage him to stop. Says psychologist and author Albert Kearney: "It is important to remember that in real-life situations, the reinforcers that shape, strengthen, and maintain target behaviors rarely occur after every instance of that behavior."[3]

7. Determine the positive reinforcers (rewards) and negative stimuli.

What reinforces Mark's biting, and what is an aversion to this behavior? The best way to determine Mark's positive reinforcers is to ask him what he likes or dislikes. You can also ask his teachers and friends. If Mark loves Pepsi, you can reward him with a cup of Pepsi for not biting Mary that day. Reinforcers for a target behavior usually begin as small, tangible rewards, such as M&Ms, soda pop, a baseball card, or a sticker, awarded throughout the day with praise for the desired behaviors. When Krystal addressed Jonathan, and he looked her in the eyes, Krystal handed Jonathan three M&Ms and said, "Good job, Jonathan!" Remember to vary reinforcements so the child does not become tired of a particular reward.

As the negative target behavior occurs less frequently, the therapist and you can begin to replace tangible rewards with the intangible reward of praise. The power of the influence of the reinforcement is referred to as *general level of reinforcement*. After a few days, your child may become tired of eating M&Ms, and you can replace that reinforcement with something new, like baseball cards. Determining positive reinforcers is crucial for developing the reward system in your child's individual ABA program.

8. Design and implement an ABA program for your child's unique needs.

How will you respond to Mark's target behavior? Using the research and data gathered, you can implement the treatment program. You should be attentive to times, locations, stimuli, or events that affect the frequency of Mark's biting. The program will focus on reinforcing the behavior you desire to increase while using extinction (negative stimuli) to weaken the undesired target behavior.

9. Monitor the program.

Once you have developed the program for Mark's situations and target behavior, put the treatment into operation. This is referred to as intervention. You can monitor the program by keeping a journal with statistics of the frequency of Mark's behavior based on his baseline. This should include both how often the target behavior happens and the duration of each occurrence. You can observe the rate of Mark's improvement based on data you have collected. Testing the result of intervention in ABA is termed *probing*. One method to test the effectiveness of the treatment is to cease it for a period of time. If the individual regresses to the pre-treatment baseline, you can confirm that the program is effective. This is called the A-B-A-B reversal design.

10. Evaluate and make adjustments to the treatment.

Through observation, you have collected new data and are able to make an assessment of Mark's treatment. Has your intervention caused Mark to bite Mary less frequently? Based on Mark's improvement, should you focus your resource in intervention on making extinct a different yet undesirable target behavior?

These are the ten simple steps of ABA therapy. (If only ABA was that easy for parents and therapists!) Some children may require forty hours a week in ABA therapy, for months or even years, before improvement is detectable. Dr. O. Ivar Lovaas, a leading pioneer of ABA therapy for autism, says:

> We were expecting a sudden step forward, that possibly somehow we would hit upon some central cognitive, emotional, or social event inside the child's mind that would help him make a sudden and major leap ahead. Traditional conceptions are filled with such promises. Such a leap would have been so gratifying, and it would

have made our work so much easier. It never happened. Instead, progress followed a slow, step-by-step upward progression, with only a few minor spurts ahead. We learned to settle down for hard work.[4]

THE ABCs OF ABA

This is a rather lengthy section, so stick with me. ABA therapy seeks to change the behaviors that directly impact the child's daily life and social skills. Some behaviors a child may display too often (behavioral excesses)—for example, flapping his hands or spinning. Other behaviors he may model too infrequently (behavioral deficits); examples are a lack of eye of contact or failing to follow directions. ABA focuses both on adapting socially unacceptable behaviors and teaching new skills.

Negative behaviors are referred to as maladaptive behavior. ABA targets such behaviors to adapt them to positive behaviors through *reinforcement*. This is a stimulus delivered immediately after a positive response or behavior is exhibited that helps increase the probability that the specific behavior will occur in the future. Reinforcements should be frequent at first and fade over time.

Three types of reinforcers are primary, secondary, and activity. *Primary reinforcers* are tangible rewards, such as food or a small toy. *Secondary reinforcers* are things like hugs and praise. *Activity reinforcers* are privileges earned by appropriate behavior, like a trip to the beach. *Token economy rewards* are attempts to increase desired behaviors by awarding tokens that can be exchanged later for rewards. You can make reinforcers more effective by using them only for the desired behavior.

I will quickly review ABA's two main types of reinforcements and punishments.

Positive reinforcement is using a motivating/reinforcing stimulus after a desired behavior is exhibited, making it more likely the behavior will occur in the future. A *stimulus* is simply something that stimulates or creates a reaction. Jonathan receives M&Ms (positive stimulus) for eye contact (behavior). The next time Krystal prompts Jonathan, he looks her in the eye, expecting to receive M&Ms.

Negative reinforcement is not punishment; instead, it is when something unpleasant is removed. The purpose of this reinforcement is for the behavior that led to the removal of the unpleasant thing to increase in the future because it created a favorable outcome.[5]

For example, let's say when the light turns green at the traffic light, the car in front of you does not move. You know from experience that blasting your horn will cause Mr. Pokey to move. So you blast your horn. Before you honked your horn, the car was not moving. So you acted by blasting the horn. Afterward the car moved. In the future, you will blast your horn to cause the cars in front of you to move. That is negative reinforcement—actions that lead to the removal of something unpleasant.

You must also be aware of how your child may be using negative reinforcement on you. For instance, let's say you're in the supermarket, and your child cries (behavior) until you buy him gum (positive stimulus). By buying your child gum (positive stimulus) to remove the unpleasant crying (behavior), you have unintentionally influenced him to repeat this negative behavior. Your child has learned that if he cries in the store, you will give him what he wants.

The two types of negative reinforcements are escape and avoidance. *Escape reinforcement* occurs when a behavior stops an existing aversive situation. Your alarm is blaring (negative stimulus), so you turn it off (behavior). *Avoidance reinforcement* is behaving a certain way to prevent negative consequences. Jonathan learned to say the word "push" (behavior) while on the swings to avoid Krystal removing him from the swings (a negative consequence). Another obvious example is that you don't use the "five-finger discount" at Walmart (behavior) for fear of being arrested (negative consequence).

Punishment adds something aversive in order to decrease a certain behavior. There are two forms of punishment: *positive punishment* is adding an aversive stimulus, and *negative punishment* is the removal of a stimulus to decrease a behavior.

Positive punishment uses a negative consequence after an unwanted behavior is displayed, making the behavior less likely to recur. In ABA this is termed *response cost*. For example, Mark bites Mary (behavior), and his therapist reprimands (negative stimulus) him. Jonathan is yelling on the swings (behavior), and Krystal removes him from his swing and makes him take a ten-minute time-out (negative stimulus).

Says ABA therapist Jas Dimitriou: "The hardest part of a therapist's job is constantly redirecting undesired behaviors. For example, when a child covers his ears, one technique you may use is to give a GMI (gross motor imitation), such as clap your hands if needed so the child is forced to remove his hands. You use a clicker to count the number of times a target behavior occurs. Sometimes in teaching a new behavior you change the child's schedule to develop flexibility and prevent repetitive structure."[6]

Negative punishment is removing a desired stimulus after an undesired behavior occurs, resulting in the behavior decreasing. For example, Mark bites Mary (behavior), and his mom takes away his video games (desired stimulus) for two days. Another example: Mary loves music class. While in class, Mary throws a book at Mark (behavior), and her mother removes Mary from music class (desired stimulus).

Research studies indicate that positive reinforcement produces better results than punishment. Adding a positive to increase a response works best and allows both parties to focus on the positive aspects of the situation. When applied immediately following a maladaptive behavior, punishment can be effective, but it may invoke other negative responses, such as anger and resentment.

Reinforcement schedules help you to know when and how to apply reinforcements. For a reinforcement to be effective, it must be accurately timed and delivered promptly after the desired behavior. The child needs to understand why he is being rewarded for his behavior. There are four types of schedules for reinforcements:

1. In a **fixed ratio schedule** the reinforcement is applied after a certain number of behaviors. Krystal removes Jonathan from swings after asking him three times to say "push" without a response.

2. In a **fixed interval schedule** the reinforcement is applied after a certain amount of time. Krystal gives Jonathan twenty minutes to say the word "push" correctly before removing him from the swings. Fixed intervals are continuously applied on a regular basis.

3. In a **variable ratio** scenario a reinforcement is applied after a variable number of responses. This schedule is like a slot machine. The child knows that the positive behavior will be rewarded, but he does not know how many times he must perform the act before obtaining results.

4. A **variable interval** scenario gives reinforcement after a variable amount of time. Your child continues his good behavior knowing that after a while his teacher will check his actions and

reward him. Variable schedules produce more consistent behaviors and stronger responses to reinforcements than fixed interval schedules. The process of switching from a continued schedule to a variable one is referred to as thinning.[7]

The ABCs of ABA are antecedent (A), behavior (B), and consequence (C). This is also referred to as the three-term contingency. If A is in place, then B occurs, and if B occurs, then C follows. The antecedent is the circumstance that preceeds the behavior; it is what triggers the behavior. The behavior is the action. As Dr. Newman so insightfully shares: "You can help with the behavior problem once you know the function of the behavior."[8]

When analyzing a target behavior, ask yourself, "What occurred before the behavior?"

What happens after the behavior occurs is the consequence. You can think of the consequence as the payoff for the behavior. A simple example of ABC applied is when Krystal instructs Jonathan to say the word *push* (A), Jonathan repeats the word *push* (B), and then Krystal responds by saying, "Great job" (C).

In the treatment plan you should clearly define the target behaviors you desire to adapt and the skills you want to teach. First, discover the baseline of the target behavior by collecting data. Then decide what reinforcers to use. Apply the ABA methods to modify behavior. Break the complex behavioral task into smaller steps, using one-on-one teaching with reinforcers until the child successfully performs the desired task. Continue this process until the behavior is performed regularly. Measure the progress based on the baseline. Fade the reinforcements slowly by thinning until they can become extinct and the desired behavior is now normal.

In the progression of ABA there will often be an *extinction burst*; the maladaptive behavior will get worse before it becomes extinct. The three ways behavior can become worse is frequency (more of the behavior), magnitude (higher intensity of the behavior), and variability (performs behavior differently).

Generalization

Many children with autism have difficulty with generalization. *Generalization* is teaching children to apply an acquired skill learned in one setting to another. You can accomplish this by applying the skill in a variety of everyday situations and under different scenarios. Krystal is teaching Jonathan to ask politely to use the swings. She will also teach him to ask politely when he wants to take a break or ride his bike. Another example of generalization is that although Jonathan first learned the word *cat* in a therapeutic environment, he is also being taught to use the term in his natural environment.

When Jackie takes her son to the zoo on Friday, she will teach Jonathan that lions and tigers are also part of the cat family. In the evening, when Jonathan's dad, Jim, takes him for a walk, Jim will point to every feline in the neighborhood and exclaim, "Look at that cat!"

Now that you have a basic understanding of ABA and its terminology, I will examine a couple of simple case studies to demonstrate how ABA is applied.

Case Study 1: Eye Contact

When people address Jonathan by name, he fails to give them eye contact. How would ABA be applied in this situation?

Step 1: Identify the target behavior you want to change: eye contact. The treatment objective is to help Jonathan develop consistent eye contact when someone speaks to him.

Step 2: Discover his baseline for eye contact. Krystal uses a clicker to make a *click* sound when the desired behavior is performed, and collects data on Jonathan's eye contact for the week. During a sample week Jonathan used eye contact only eight times out of two hundred occasions, which is only 4 percent. Of the eight times, the duration of eye contact was an average of 1.5 seconds. The goal is have Jonathan use eye contact consistently and with at least a 3-second duration.

Step 3: Develop the positive reinforcers that will encourage the desired behavior. Jonathan loves baseball. Krystal will give him one baseball card each time he looks at her when addressed and two cards if he looks at her for at least three seconds.

Step 4: Intervene by implementing a program of the appropriate ABA techniques.

Step 5: Monitor the program. Krystal continues to observe and collect data. After three days Jonathan gives eye contact seventy times out of a hundred, a 66 percent improvement. After a week Krystal begins using the thinning method. For every five times Jonathan gives eye contact for at least three seconds, Krystal gives him a baseball card.

Step 6: Evaluate and make adjustments. Krystal reanalyzed the data and discovered that Jonathan now makes eye contact for three seconds (or longer) more than 95 percent of the time. Allow the data to guide the decision-making progress. Jonathan's treatment program is adjusted to fade the reinforcements into extinction over the next two weeks. Krystal and the ABA team meet again with Jim and Jackie to determine the next behavior to target.

CASE STUDY 2: BITING

Mark bites his sister, Mary, on her arm, leaving welts. How would ABA be applied in this situation?

Step 1: Identify the target behavior—Mark biting Mary's arm.

Step 2: Discover Mark's baseline for biting. Krystal has Mary record in a journal every time she is bitten. Mark bit Mary's arm ten times during the week.

Step 3: Identify the antecedents. Five of the ten times Mark bit Mary were before lunch, and four times were before dinner. The final time was right before his bedtime.

Step 4: Record the location of behavior. Three times Mark bit Mary in the kitchen, two times in his bedroom, and five times in the living room.

Step 5: Record the time of the biting.

Step 6: Identify the consequence. Mary screamed at Mark and chased him around the house.

Step 7: Determine the proper positive reinforcers (rewards) and negative stimuli. Mark loves video games. For every four hours Mark goes without biting Mary, he will receive a token. For every two tokens Mark receives, he will be allowed to play video games for a half hour. After Mark receives forty tokens, his parents will buy him a new game. As a negative stimulus, if Mark bites Mary, his parents will take away his video games for the night.

Step 8: Implement the plan using ABA. The first day Mark does not bite Mary, and he receives a half hour of video game play. The second day Mark bites Mary twice. So he loses the privilege of playing video games for two nights (negative punishment).

Step 9: Monitor the program. Mary continues to record the frequency and duration of Mark's bites.

Step 10: Evaluate and make adjustments. With data collected by Mary, Krystal determines that over the last two weeks Mark's biting decreased 30 percent. She will continue the intervention and reevaluate the data in a week. When Mark's biting decreases to only 5 percent, she will begin the process of thinning and fading his reinforcements. Wrote blogger Brian King: "As you introduce new strategies with your child living with ADHD or ASD, keep in mind that it's rare for any new approach to work perfectly out of the gate. Tweaking is almost always necessary. Be mindful of any feelings of failure that creep in. All results are useful. They tell us what's working and what we need to work on."[9]

PLAYTIME THERAPY

Therapy is most effective in the child's natural environment and during his or her playtime. Occupational therapist and author Beth Aune—the founder of Desert Occupational Therapy for Kids—told me, "Children learn social skills best during floortime as they interact with each other through playing."[10] In *A Practical Guide to Autism*, coauthors Fred Volkmar and Lisa Wiesner note that play helps children develop more sophisticated ways of thinking:

> [Play] is the beginning of being able to imagine how things could be and to be able to take the world apart and put it right back together, sometimes in very creative ways. Because play is also very symbolic, it is intimately related to language development. For the typical developing child then, play opens up whole new worlds and the child learns to seek new experiences from which he or she can learn.[11]

SELF-MANAGEMENT

The ultimate goal of ABA therapy is to improve the child's ability to manage and control his or her own emotions and behavior. "Self-management is one of the most advanced techniques in ABA," says Dr. Newman. "When a student learns to self-manage, he or she learns to watch his or her behavior and deliver reinforcers in keeping with that behavior."[12]

A Christian therapist will also stress the need for the child to control his or her impulses and emotions, using both ABA techniques and the power of the Holy Spirit. As the Apostle Paul wrote, "But the fruit of the Spirit is love, joy, peace, patience, gentleness, goodness, faith, meekness, and self-control" (Gal. 5:22–23, MEV).

Self-management includes teaching children to recognize when they are having difficulty and ask for help, while also giving them opportunities to make different choices. The goal is to independently help them learn to calm down, as well as monitor and change their own behavior. Explains Linda Hodgdon, a behavioral expert on autism: "Long-term goal of self-management is to teach students strategies that will help them handle themselves appropriately in difficult situations. Giving them some rules and direction guides them to make appropriate behavior choices during stressful or upsetting incidents."[13]

SUMMARY

As you have learned, ABA does not produce instant results but is a slow process that brings transformation. In ABA, therapists and parents choose the target behaviors they hope to correct and the specific skills they want the child to learn. A treatment plan is developed according to the child's unique needs and is applied with reinforcers. The therapist and parents use the ten steps of ABA and collect data for results. ABA is most effective when applied both at home and in the community. As you have seen, ABA is hard work. Friends can help you by offering you a break from your child's therapy routine.

STORIES FROM THE HEART

THIS CHAPTER INCLUDES seven original personal stories. Written by well-known authors and professionals in the autism community, they share the author's faith and life experiences with autism.

While I was interviewing Beth Aune on the topic of autism and therapy, she shared with me Elizabeth's amazing testimony of her first Communion. Among other things, this story demonstrates the importance of faith, coupled with therapy, to help children develop social skills.

FIRST HOLY COMMUNION: A SPECIAL GIRL'S SPIRITUAL JOURNEY

As a pediatric occupational therapist, I am blessed to work with and share experiences with multitudes of children with autism and to travel with their parents as a welcome guest and source of support as their child explores and grows during their earthly journey. Sometimes the journey is a brief one, but in Elizabeth's case, it began before she was two years old and diagnosed with "severe autism." It continued as she prepared to enter fifth grade in a general-education setting at a private Catholic school.

Our work and therapy together is dynamic and fluid, addressing Elizabeth's challenges through her developmental progress and the incorporation of her developing gifts and talents.

Through the years many gifted and dedicated family members, educators, and therapists have traveled this journey with Elizabeth and me. Yet the consistent ties that bind us include her mother, SueAnn, our shared faith in God, and the Spirit that is so alive in Elizabeth.

Occupational therapists believe the child must be treated in the context of his or her environment. We base our treatment plans and approaches to address the concerns of the child, her parents, and her teachers. We provide therapy, support, and strategies to help a child with autism to regulate sensory and behavioral responses, develop gross and fine motor skills, increase independence in self-care, improve feeding and eating behavior, deepen and foster play and social interaction, and enhance self-image and self-confidence in their abilities.

Elizabeth has been working on all these areas of occupational performance, and her progress has been simply amazing, thanks to the combined efforts of her village of dedicated and faith-filled individuals.

However, it is Elizabeth herself, and the Spirit that lives within her, that is the guide and strength for her journey. When Elizabeth was in second grade, she and her classmates began preparations for their first Holy Communion. SueAnn's two older children, Victoria and Chris, had attended the same school and participated in this important spiritual experience. So it was SueAnn's dream and desire for her youngest daughter to understand and experience this spiritual milestone.

There were some serious obstacles to address, but SueAnn and I knew in our hearts that Elizabeth could and would overcome those obstacles with support. With the gifts and talents of Wendy, her faith-filled educational therapist, Elizabeth gained a deeper comprehension of the lessons and scripts she memorized under the tutelage of her teacher.

Her priest allowed me to attend her first confession. He incorporated the strategy of asking closed-ended and concrete questions rather than open-ended, abstract questions to elicit a confession of her transgressions. His staff provided unconsecrated Communion wafers so we could, over several months, simulate and practice confession during occupational therapy and help her take and eat the wafer.

SueAnn purchased her beautiful, white dress months in advance. Elizabeth wore it at home to get used to the sensation of the clothing. The school staff provided numerous opportunities to go through the routine inside the church. When the special day arrived, Elizabeth was extremely excited but also very anxious. I remember sitting with her in the pew, taking deep breaths, and praying for peace. I felt calm and confident that Elizabeth was prepared. Watching her walk with her classmates and approach the priest with joy and excitement as she took Communion while he blessed her—that was a moment that will forever be etched in my heart.

I've asked Elizabeth's mom, SueAnn, to also share her perspective on this event:

From the moment Elizabeth was born, I knew she was special. Born three weeks early with a head full of black hair that stuck straight up, she was already making her presence known as unique and different from her two blonde siblings. Her diagnosis of autism around the age of two years old just confirmed her individuality in our family.

"She will probably need to be institutionalized when she's older," experts said. Since Elizabeth was a child who didn't use words and made no eye contact (and who screamed when in unfamiliar surroundings and ate baby food until she was five), I almost believed them—but just for a moment. God had other plans for her—bigger plans. Through her strong spirit and the tight-knit village constructed uniquely for her, Elizabeth has shown everyone that she is not only able, but she is also soaring.

Through her challenges, her accomplishments, and her heart, God has humbled me and made me a better mother and a better human. I am eternally grateful for Beth Aune, who was the first person who answered honestly when I asked, "Do you think she's autistic?" Beth has been my rock, as well as Elizabeth's guardian angel, guiding us on this journey that I never anticipated for our life but would never change. Life is a dance, and Elizabeth is just beginning to show us all the great moves she has in store for the world.

Indeed, today what Elizabeth knows about God can be summed up in a brief declaration: "God is love. God is perfect. He loves me so much, and He makes me feel happy."

Beth Aune is the founder of Desert Occupational Therapy for Kids and author of three books.

SueAnn Lundberg Etebar is an RN case manager of nephrology and transplant at Desert Oasis Healthcare.

USING SPECIAL INTERESTS TO BUILD COMMUNICATION

When I interviewed Lois Brady, I was amazed at her practical insight into developing children's social and communication skills, so I asked her to write a short story sharing her wisdom. Her insights remind me of the way my mom used art, animals, and other fun activities to spark my interest in learning.

Challenges with communication are at the core of autism. As a speech-language pathologist and mom, I spend countless hours at work and home, building effective communication skills.

This is what I have learned over the years: every child on the autism spectrum is unique. An individualized, personal approach to communication that fits both the child and his or her family should be designed with the child's special interests in mind.

For example, I use Buttercup, my potbelly pig, to connect with students who love animals. Many of my students feel comfortable talking with an animal. In fact, they may say their first words to an animal. The communication skills used when talking with a pet can ultimately be transferred to a human.[1]

Another child may be motivated by music, songs, and movement. So we sing and dance to communicate. The melody and dance steps are incrementally faded as the student communicates.

The use of technology has made a *huge* impact, motivating children with autism to communicate and learn. Touch-screen devices have not only given children a way to express themselves but are changing expectations of children on the spectrum. Traditional ways of using technology are being replaced by highly motivating methods, such as apps and iPads. My extensive experience working and living with children on the spectrum has given me the insights to build a communication app (www.innervoiceapp.com), which uses motivation and special interests to build communication.

My son—who loved to line up his cars through the living room, down the hall, and into the kitchen—learned the important skill of communication during activity driven by new technologies. We spent hundreds of hours working together, placing cars bumper to bumper as we created the world's largest traffic jam. I kept the cars in a large bucket; if he wanted one, he had to ask for it. Initially he just said, "Car," then, "Blue

car," and then, "Shiny blue car." Eventually he was able
to tell me where the car was going, find the location on
the map, and finally spell the location both on the key-
board and by freehand. He thought we were playing, but
I knew we were doing something that would give him
lifelong skills in language and literacy.

Creating a communication system for children on the
autism spectrum is a unique challenge for every family.
My advice in a nutshell is this: use your child's special
interests (animals, music, technology, cars, etc.) to go
into his or her world, and slowly lead the child to yours.

Lois Joan Brady, MA, CCC-SLP, is the developer and
producer of *Autism Today TV* and the author of three
books on autism.

THE EIGHTEEN-INCH MIRACLE

During my conversation with Cynthia Cournoyer, I was
moved by the journey of faith her daughter, Jenny, who has
Asperger's, has taken. Jenny's testimony beautifully communicates the gospel message to literal thinkers with autism and
the importance of a relationship with Christ.

It's a myth that people with autism cannot understand
God and therefore cannot have a relationship with Him.
People say things like, "God is too abstract of a concept";
"Theology is not concrete"; or, "Belief in God isn't logical."
While it is true that some people with autism are athe-
ists, there are also atheists who are not autistic. It's also a
myth that people with autism can't understand the feel-
ings of others. We can learn. I did.

I prayed the prayer of salvation when I was nineteen
years old. Yes, I live on the ASD spectrum, and I have a
relationship with Jesus Christ. It is possible. Wonderful
Christian friends who deeply cared for me showed me

the love and forgiveness of Christ. I was probably like many stories of salvation that you've heard: I realized and understood that I was a sinner who needed grace and forgiveness. I learned that Jesus Christ was willing to die for me, and He did. All I had to do was open the door to my heart and let Him in.

I was never discouraged from knowing about God. I grew up hearing Bible stories. The idea of one all-powerful, ever-present, all-knowing Creator who made everything in the universe made sense. In fact, that was a very logical thought for an autistic person. (Actually, the thought of a random universe is quite illogical.)

People with autism desire predictability: a place for everything and everything in its place. However, believing that there is a God is very different from believing that you need to have an intimate relation-ship with God. That's the eighteen-inch miracle—when it goes from your head to your heart.

What is true about people with autism is that we take things very literally. We read something, memo-rize it, and apply it as part of the "building materials" that we use to construct and make sense of the world. The Creation story in the Bible can be a part of these materials. So can the stories about Noah's ark, Abraham, Isaac, Jacob, the Exodus, and the kings of Israel. All the way through the birth, death, and resurrection of Jesus, Bible stories contain value. Because ASD children with faith know the "building materials" so well, in a way, you can say we have an even stronger foundation of faith. As it says in 1 Samuel 16:7, "The LORD looks at the heart."

The heart—emotion. Feeling. Suffering. Grace. Forgiveness. Hope. These abstract concepts can some-times be difficult for a person with autism to understand. But grasping them is not impossible. All things are pos-sible with God. A friend of mine in high school once pointed out to me that I was afraid of my own heart. He was right. I didn't understand my own heart. All people are afraid of what they don't understand. I had plenty of head knowledge of the Bible, but knowledge is useless without love. God is love. And on one cold December night the Holy Spirit spoke to my heart when I asked Him the question: "What am I supposed to know?" His answer was clear: "You're supposed to know Me." It was in that moment that all the Bible knowledge made sense in my heart and not just my head. That was my eighteen-inch miracle.

Jenny Thomas is a young adult with Asperger's who earned a master of arts degree in teaching from Western Oregon University. She taught middle and high school social studies and Spanish for six years at public and private Christian schools. Jenny and her husband, Randall, now work for a nonprofit organization that provides support for adults with developmental disabilities.

GOD'S PRESENCE

Kathleen Deyer Bolduc is a regular blogger at Not Alone, a website for special-needs parenting, where I also contribute articles. When I interviewed Kathleen, I enjoyed hearing how God's grace and love have been at work in her life as she has raised her son Joel. Here she shares her journey.

The Word became flesh and blood, and moved into the neighborhood.

—JOHN 1:14, THE MESSAGE

I think I really began to understand how much God wants to pitch a tent within our neighborhood after our third son, Joel, was born in 1985. Have you ever sat on the beach, on that part of the sand where the waves have just receded, where the sand is damp and packed down tightly? You take a plastic shovel, or perhaps your hand, and begin to dig. You dig and dig until water begins to burble up from within the sand, finally filling the hole you've carefully carved out.

The poet Kahlil Gibran writes, "Your joy is your sorrow unmasked.... The deeper the sorrow carves into your being, the more joy you can contain."[2] I know what it is to grieve—parents of children with disabilities know what experts call "chronic grief." Joel has autism and moderate intellectual disabilities. He also has an anxiety disorder and severe kyphosis (excessive curvature) of the spine.

After Joel's birth I had to rethink and reevaluate everything I valued in life, such as the value of intelligence, efficiency, logic, and self-control. The old rules no longer applied. My spirit, which craved peace, order, comfort, and security, withered as I struggled to make sense of the seemingly senseless—a beautiful boy with an impaired brain. I was stuck in denial for a very long time. When I finally broke free, I raced headlong into anger, self-blame, and depression.

Throughout this grieving process I never stopped calling out to God. Even on my darkest days, when my mind was too numb to form a prayer, I repeated three words over and over: *Help me, Lord!* The grief itself became my prayer. Those years of lament carved a space in my parched spirit for God's living waters.

The details of life with Joel did not change. The result of his neurological disability caused behaviors that were very difficult to deal with—hair pulling, tantrums, and an inability to be in large groups of people or to tolerate certain noises. His cognitive disability made learning the easiest of tasks difficult. But the life-giving waters began to flow as I caught fleeting glimpses of reasons to rejoice in the midst of it all: Joel's infectious grin, his silly jokes ("Turkey fell off the waterfall and bumped his head!"), his compassion for people who were hurting ("Wanna pray for him!"), his unconditional love, and his contagious joy in worship.

I had long struggled to fit prayer and meditation into my busy life. Suddenly it was no longer a struggle. I simply made the time because the waters that welled up in the silence filled me to overflowing.

The dry soil of my life became hydrated and led me to testify, through the written word, about the ways God has redeemed Joel's broken places, as well as my brokenness. He filled our weakness with His strength. God also led me to two sisters in Christ, with whom I pray every Wednesday morning. He led me to regular times of retreat. He led my husband and me to begin our own contemplative retreat center, where we offer prayer, praise, and spiritual direction on a weekly basis. God also led us to help establish a thriving farm—a community where Joel could thrive as an adult (http://www .safehavenfarms.org/).

In the words of the poet Wendell Berry, "It gets darker and darker, and then Jesus is born."[3] Living with Joel has been an incredible journey in patience, trust, and obedience. Most of all, it assured us that the Lord had pitched a tent in our neighborhood—within us, above us, behind us, and in front of us, every step of the way. So, many years later, I give thanks daily for the most important spiritual teacher of my life: my son Joel.

Kathleen Deyer Bolduc, MA, is a nationally recognized author and speaker in the field of disability and spirituality. Her books include *The Spiritual Art of Raising Children With Disabilities, Autism & Alleluias, A Place Called Acceptance: Ministry With Families of Children With Disabilities,* and *His Name is Joel: Searching for God in a Son's Disability.* She writes as the mother of an adult son with autism and as a spiritual director. Visit Kathy's website at http://www.kathleenbolduc.com.

THRIVING WITH AUTISM

Many parents think of autism as a life sentence with which they must cope, which is why I love Craig Evans's concept of thriving with autism. I think his perspective could be a source of inspiration for many, so I've asked him to share his insights here.

When I first met my future stepson, I was deeply awed by two things: his extraordinary gifts and his debilitating challenges. I wondered, "How will such a remarkable, creative human being find his way in life?" For this to happen, I knew one prerequisite was in order: a good attitude. So, I began my search for hopeful inspiration.

Oddly enough, in 2003, I discovered a scarcity of good, positive attitudes toward autism online. Doom and discouragement seemed to reign! At best, I found a benign attitude of just plain "we don't know." As a perpetually glass "half-full" person wanting to assist my future stepson and those like him, I knew I needed to change that.

My career had been as a communications professional. I had built many websites and constructed and produced marketing campaigns for major brands. In 2008 I used those skills to build AutismHangout.com, with the intent of finding and promoting positive, hopeful messages for those living with autism—and the families, caretakers, teachers, and others ministering to them. The good news is: I didn't have to look far to find them. I hitched up my computer and video camera so that I could record my interviews (conducted via Skype) and post them to YouTube for all to see. That launched my career as a journalist.

I learned when contacting guests for interviews that the authors, experts, teachers, professionals, and community service people I approached had never done such a thing. So they mostly agreed to participate! Within a few months I had conducted discussions with the most forward-thinking people in the autism field. Within a few years I had captured more than two hundred of these positive, hopeful programs. When we built our inventory to more than five hundred videos, about half had been posted by the website's membership! Clearly I found I was not alone in the quest not just to survive with autism but *thrive!* The best news is that our special kids and their families are succeeding! Indeed, a good attitude has helped.

As people on the autism spectrum age, there is mounting evidence that thriving is not just possible; in fact, it's highly probable! *Many* people gifted with aspects of autism—such as excellent memory, attention to detail, the incredible ability to focus, and more—provide the evidence. The examples include the twenty-eight "Aspie Mentors" assembled for my book *Been There. Done That. Try This!*, which I co-authored with Dr. Tony Attwood, the world's leading authority on Asperger's, and Aspie mentor Anita Lesko!

Today, my message remains the same—a good attitude is in order. Thriving with autism is a realistic, satisfying, achievable goal. I wish you and your loved ones a life filled with good thriving!

Craig Evans is an internationally known autism advocate and coauthor of *Been There. Done That. Try This!: An Aspie's Guide to Life on Earth.*

Overcoming the World

In 2014 I met Kelli Ra Anderson at a writer's conference in Wheaton, Illinois. I was so encouraged by her story of raising two sons with autism and so inspired by her faith in Christ that I asked her to share her journey.

We knew there was something special about our first child soon after he was born. At six months he spoke his first word. By eighteen months of age he spoke in complete sentences and (much to the delight of onlookers in grocery stores) enthusiastically shouted out the oversized numbers he recognized at checkout counters. I would like to say it was a result of my superlative teaching skills as a new mother, but not even *Sesame Street* can take the credit for the abilities we could not explain.

Even more remarkable was the morning I opened a new coloring book, and my two-year-old pointed to the word at the bottom of the page and said, "Black." I did a double take. As I turned the pages, he correctly identified the next word and the next. By preschool, tests showed him reading at a ninth-grade level.

However, as time moved on, he also displayed increasingly odd behaviors. During second grade we learned why. As my husband and I sat across the desk from a pediatric neuropsychologist, we heard "autism" and "Asperger's syndrome," words that expelled him from his private school and propelled us into a world no one really understood. However, from the beginning of John's exceptional life, God has been hard at work. For the last two decades we have continued to learn the life-giving lessons of humility, identity, forgiveness, and trust. We carved these qualities out of hardships caused by ignorance, judgment, false hopes, false gods, and false identity.

As a woman who found her self-worth in performance,

it is a regrettable fact that overachievement and hiding my flaws represented a way of life. But autism does not hide or bow to the god of expectations. And in a Christian worldview that credits and applauds those who sire an obedient child, there is seldom room for understanding, grace, or mercy for those whose children don't easily conform. It meant there was no longer room to serve the idol I had created in my own image.

The diagnosis of our second son with Asperger's syndrome, and then ADHD in our daughter, turned my spiritual world upside down. But it wasn't until I raised the white flag of surrender, under the crushing weight of problems I didn't know how to heal or hide, that God was finally able to transform the idol of self. In its place came a real life with Him that is continuing to change just about everything about me (except, maybe, my penchant for L'Oreal).

In the years since, daily reliance on God—spending honest time with Him to let Him care for me so I may better care for my family—has been an anchor in a sometimes tumultuous sea. However, I am learning that my value, and that of my children, is not found in achievements applauded by *People* magazine (or even the church), but in being deeply and completely loved by the Abba Father, who made us for His purpose and for joy in the midst of our messes.

I am learning to receive forgiveness from God (for my maddeningly slow learning curve), to ask my children to forgive me (for flawed parenting and PMS), and to extend forgiveness to those who have been uncaring, unkind, and judgmental. Grace is a three-way street.

And I am learning to trust. Mercifully, as the rear-view picture of our lives grows larger, I see more and more how God has gently taken and transformed what we lay at His feet. I can see better how aspects of autism are a true blessing—and how He is allowing us to be a blessing to others. As He did with the horror and absurdity of the cross, God transforms what seems hopelessly broken and breathes into it new, life-giving purpose. Yes, in this life we will have trouble; Jesus foretold that in John 16:33. But then He added the words that change everything: "But take heart! I have overcome the world."

Kelli Ra Anderson is a writer for several national magazines, a blogger, speaker, and author. She lives in Illinois with her husband of twenty-five years, their three young adult children—two of whom have autism—and one slightly obnoxious Goldendoodle. For more information, visit her website, www.kellira.com.

UNDERSTANDING EVERYDAY LIVES

I was humbled to interview Dr. Lynn Koegel, one of the foremost experts on autism treatment, and inspired by her story of Joe, a young college student with Asperger's. Having Asperger's myself, I could appreciate Joe's struggles with relationships and understand his desire to meet new people. Following is an interview Dr. Koegel conducted with Joe focusing on his experience learning new social skills through applied behavioral therapy.

Dr. Koegel: One in every five thousand students gets a perfect score on the SAT. Joe did that without studying. That doesn't seem fair to the students who spend countless hours sweating over study guides, vocabulary lists, and math equations. But while the other students were dealing with pressures over what score they would achieve and what options they would have for college, Joe had other burdens that were far more challenging than the SAT.

Joe: I have Asperger's syndrome. During my formative years I had just enough self-awareness to realize that I often came across as being a bit odd. However, at the time I did not possess the ability to analyze my own actions and ascertain what precisely it was about me that people found to be off-putting. But I did realize that keeping quiet was a fairly safe bet for avoiding embarrassment. So I quickly made it my *modus operandi*.

Looking back, the first signs of my social withdrawal may have manifested as early as age five. By age seven or eight my lack of sociability was set in stone. Unfortunately the problem seemed to compound over time. As my peers' social skills grew rapidly, thanks to constant usage, mine improved at a much slower rate due to a lack of practice.

Dr. Koegel: I didn't know Joe when he was growing up, but he was most likely a victim of people's lack of understanding of how important socialization is in the young years. It's hard for me to understand why everyone panics and seeks help and tutoring right away if a child is having trouble learning to read or finds math challenging. But too few people seem to worry if a child plays by himself or isolates herself. In fact, it's frightening how often I hear, "He doesn't want to socialize, so we're not going to push him," or, "Every child gets to choose what he or she wants to do at recess, and he chooses to be alone."

All parents want their child to have friends and get along with others, and some children need a little extra help to reach that end. A complete social evaluation in a natural setting with peers should be an integral part of every child's curriculum. If a child isn't socializing or is having trouble making friends, a treatment program should be considered immediately.

Joe: It seems so obvious now that heading off to a college where I did not know anyone and did not have any sort of support system was a recipe for disaster. But if I have learned anything during my time on this earth, it's that it is very difficult to have an objective and rational view of a situation if you are constantly and fervently wishing that the realities of the situation were markedly different.

On that note—despite a total lack of evidence that I was even remotely equipped to succeed—my parents and I agreed that I would go across the country to attend Duke University. Predictably, my excursion to North Carolina was a disaster. I essentially did not interact with anyone except my roommate. On the day of my first chemistry lab I couldn't find the right room and could not bring myself to ask anyone for directions.

The prospect of having to explain to the professor or a teaching assistant what had happened left me in abject terror. So I just stopped going to class. This pattern of behavior soon extended to every aspect of the college experience. I began staying in my room almost all the time, typically leaving only to eat.

After midterms came and went, my parents were notified that I had not taken any exams and was not attending any of my classes. The school granted me a medical withdrawal, and I left before Thanksgiving. I returned to Duke the following fall and managed to make it through a full academic year. However, even though I managed a modicum of academic success, my social issues were still unresolved. At the start of the next academic year, old patterns reemerged, and again I had to withdraw.

Not surprisingly, depression (which has always been a serious issue for me) reared its head in a far more profound way than I had ever experienced in the past. Suicide went from being something I passively considered to something I actively planned. Fortunately at this point my mother read an article about a pilot program at the University of California at Santa Barbara for young adults with high-functioning autism.

She suggested that it might be worth looking into, although I was initially reluctant. I had already gone through years of various types of therapy that had provided no benefit whatsoever. Naturally I felt extremely pessimistic about the potential upside of trying yet another method. Still, my always-persistent mother eventually convinced me to give it a shot.

Dr. Koegel: The Koegel Autism Center operated the program; it was a dream to work with Joe. Motivation is such a big part of an adult's progress, and Joe was unquestionably motivated. He desperately wanted to have friends, a girlfriend, and a happy and fulfilling social life. In regard to accomplishing his goals, we started out videotaping him during conversations with peers and noticed that he had difficulty keeping the conversation going, in good part due to him never asking questions.

Some of his responses to social areas were acceptable. So if someone said, "I went to a great concert last weekend," he easily replied with, "Oh, that's great." Yet he didn't carry the conversation further by asking questions like, "What concert was it?" or, "What kind of music do you like?" Because he was a super nice, good-looking guy, he sometimes garnered signs of interest from females. Yet, by his own admission, maintaining their attention was extremely problematic. People want to know that their conversational partner is interested in them, what they're talking about, and how they're feeling. If you don't ask any questions, the conversation stalls and becomes one-sided. This is something that many individuals on the autism spectrum just don't pick up naturally, but it is an area where—with intervention—they can improve.

Joe: As you might imagine, given the name of my coauthor, my experience at the Koegel Center turned out to be highly beneficial. In my opinion, the primary reason the pilot program was extremely helpful for me was that it was so practical and could be applied in real-life situations. Rather than talking about my feelings regarding social interactions and setting vague goals that I would never seriously attempt to achieve, my time at the Koegel Center focused on practicing interaction in realistic social scenarios. It also analyzed the interactions to determine what worked and what did not.

A few aspects of the program turned out to be particularly helpful. Learning to engage in appropriate question asking was perhaps the most important piece of the puzzle. When conversing with someone, repeatedly asking questions about them, their ideas, and their experiences effectively shifts a substantial portion of the conversational burden onto the other person, without making the questioner seem shy or quiet.

This notion seems intuitively obvious when written out, but I can assure you that it had never occurred to me previously. Presently, although my social abilities have evolved far beyond needing to stick to a set script of asking questions, this technique remains a valuable tool for me in the case that a conversation stalls.

Dr. Koegel: Four sessions. That's all it took to see a dramatic improvement. We had Joe watch the video clips of himself talking with peers, and then we practiced having him decide what questions to ask and when to ask them. After he demonstrated proficiency with a clinician, we went on a few social outings to practice in real-life situations. A support person offered feedback and subtle prompts when appropriate ("I wonder what she thought about that professor?"). Understanding the major cause of Joe's difficulties and implementing a focused intervention made an enormous difference in making his social interactions successful.

Joe: Along similar lines, another important piece of instruction was to change the way I answered questions. Rather than respond with simple "yes" and "no" answers that impeded discourse, I learned to say "Yes, and…" and, "Not only that, but…" and then elaborate on the topic. Again, this concept probably seems simple to most people reading this, but it was a revelation to me.

Dr. Koegel: Once Joe had become comfortable and proficient at asking questions, we began practicing adding pieces of information while responding to keep the conversation going with a nice back-and-forth flow. (With adults who talk excessively, we sometimes have to work on adding fewer pieces of information.) Finally we pointed out some pragmatic behaviors, such as some awkward hand movements and posturing that were clear in the videotapes. Joe was able to self-manage those behaviors so that he fell into the typical range of what we all do at times, but it took practice and feedback.

Joe: The third practical piece of advice that was immensely helpful had to do with eliminating my fidgeting habit in social situations. To this day I still have a tendency to play with my ear or scratch my neck when I feel uncomfortable in a social situation, but it's nothing in comparison to the level of my past squirming and hand-wringing.

Once again, it may seem apparent to most readers that this is detrimental behavior, but others had to repeatedly point it out before I realized the magnitude of the problem. The dispensation of practical advice was only part of the equation. The Koegel Center's pilot program included an intensive video-modeling portion that, for me, turned out to be even more important than the specific content of the instruction I had received. Being forced to watch tape of myself struggling through simulated social interactions provided more insights than could ever be attained via basic teaching methods.

Watching myself was often truly painful. At times I wanted to leap through the video monitor and slap myself for being so impossibly awkward. But, despite wanting to cover my eyes and ears for a substantial portion of these sessions, the process triggered many broader realizations that enabled me to attain the level of social functionality I now enjoy.

Dr. Koegel: After intervention, Joe moved into a house with a group of college students with whom he interacted socially. He got a job tutoring and, after graduation, attended graduate school. While he hasn't found the perfect match, he has had no problem getting girlfriends, and some relationships have been long-term. Although I don't envy the challenges he experienced, many great things about Joe probably stem from his Asperger's.

He's super smart—so smart that many of his professors describe him as the most intelligent student they have ever had. He's the world's nicest person. He's not judgmental, and he's honest in a good way. And now that he is able to have social relationships, others who are lucky enough to have him for a friend can relish the many gifts he brings to the friendship.

Joe: To sum up my situation, the applied behavioral therapy that I received from the Koegel Center was immensely helpful. Improving my social skills was not a panacea that cured all of my ills. But without this improvement, I do not see a way I could have attained the general level of happiness and life satisfaction that I enjoy today.

—DR. LYNN KOEGEL AND JOE GARAND

Lynn K. Koegel, PhD, is the coauthor of the best seller *Overcoming Autism* and *Pivotal Response Treatments for Autism*. Dr. Koegel is one of the foremost experts on the treatment of autism and founder of the Autism Research Center at the University of California at Santa Barbara.

Joe Garand is a young adult with Apserger's who achieved a perfect score on the SAT and learned valuable social skills through applied behavioral therapy.

SUMMARY

These seven stories each teach the importance of faith and therapy in helping your child develop communication and social skills. I pray each account will give you hope and encouragement. As you trust your child in God's hands and give your unconditional love and support, you also will have a testimony to share of God's goodness and grace. As Psalm 106:2 says, "Who can proclaim the mighty acts of the LORD or fully declare his praise?"

Chapter 10

MY JOURNEY WITH AUTISM

CAN BEST DESCRIBE my struggles with autism by relating the story of an unfortunate seal named Sally. On 3/24/89 the *Exxon Valdez* oil tanker ran aground in Prince William Sound in Alaska. The ship carried approximately fifty-three million gallons of crude oil. Within a few days eleven million gallons of goo had contaminated the bay. More than eleven thousand Alaska residents and many Exxon employees worked 24/7 to restore the environment.

After spending some two billion dollars on cleansing the sea and coastline, Exxon devised a crafty plan to raise contributions for cleaning up the wildlife. The company's ingenious plan involved contributing $10,000 to a group of specialists, who would use the money to clean up one lucky seal. After this purification rite the group would use her as a mascot to raise funds to help sanitize the rest of the unfortunate victims. The specialists named their rehabilitated mascot "Sally the Seal." They even constructed a cool waterslide to help her slip back into the deep.

Then they invited television networks, dignitaries, and celebrities to witness Sally's return to her native environs. Dignitaries told reporters, "Sally the Seal will be back!" Finally Sally the Seal's big splash arrived; every camera focused on her as she slid into the sea. Suddenly a killer whale surfaced. In an instant Sally the Seal became Sally the Meal!

I often use that humorous story when I speak at high

schools and colleges because in the past, my autism often caused me to feel like Sally the Meal. I would experience great breakthroughs in school, relationships, and my career, only to get blindsided by killer whales of rejection. Sally the Seal was an easy target for predators because she, unlike other wildlife, stood out—she was the only sea creature not covered in oil. Killer whales could smell her from miles away.

Likewise, during my middle school years predator bullies' sonar systems could detect me in a crowd. With autism causing me to display unusual behavior, I represented easy prey. During a track meet in my freshman year of high school, a teammate stole a tarantula and placed it in a plastic bag. When another teammate "double-dog dared" me, I used a shot put to brew up tarantula soup. After the jock who stole the tarantula saw that I had smashed his prize, he struck me with his fist in the stomach. The next day this jock's best friend gave me a black eye.

Even after I had graduated from Oral Roberts University with a straight-A average, my autistic oddities and quirks caused me to act differently. When I became a pastor, I didn't fit most congregants' traditional image of a minister. Unlike most pastors, I had poor eye contact and at times would ramble on with personal stories. I also interpreted everything literally and appeared aloof. Yet, thanks to God's grace and favor—and help from family and friends—I have been able to overcome my autistic oddities, silence the mockers, and achieve success.[1]

Demonstrating competence helped. As author John Elder Robison says in his book *Be Different*:

> Competence excuses strange behavior. That's a very important point for us on the spectrum, because our special interests can make us extremely competent in whatever we find fascinating. At the same time,

our Asperger's often makes us look pretty strange to outsiders.[2]

OPEN DOORS

God opened new doors of opportunities when I met a minister I'll call "Pastor Larry." After I had just purchased books for the final year of my master's degree program at ORU, I hurried to the dorm to unpack the rest of my belongings. As the elevator door closed behind me, I saw a middle-aged man dressed in a stylish suit and surrounded by cardboard boxes belonging to his son. Extending his hand, he said, "Hey. I'm Pastor Larry. I'm helping my son, who is a freshman, to move into his dorm."

"Nice to meet you," I replied. "Where are you from?"

"I am pastor at a church in the metro Detroit area," he said with a smile.

"Wow, that's where I'm from!"

"My son is a preacher," Pastor Larry said. "He's studying to be a minister and evangelist."

Pastor Larry's son and I soon became friends. We both share a passion and a call to evangelism and mission ministries.

During the summer after graduation, a classmate invited me to his wedding in southeastern Michigan. He was marrying another ORU grad, and both had been students of mine while I served as a teaching assistant. As the ceremony began, I recognized the powerful voice of the presiding minister: Pastor Larry. Afterward he invited me to visit the young adult group at his church.

At the young adult service for Pastor Larry's church I reconnected with another old friend I met my freshman year at Michigan Christian College (now Rochester College). Ironically this friend was now the church's minister of young adults. After the young adult service I told him I was hoping to work in the ministry. He replied, "You should be an intern at our church." Soon after, Pastor Larry offered me a position as a volunteer intern there.

GOD'S TRAINING SCHOOL

While serving as an unpaid intern, I worked part-time as a telemarketer. The position helped me develop my communication capabilities and self-confidence, skills that served me well as I conducted more than eighty telephone interviews during the writing of this book. (As Oswald Chambers wrote in his best-selling devotional, *My Utmost for His Highest*, "God works where He sends us to wait."[3])

Ironically the same week the church offered me a full-time paid position as intern of ministry, my part-time employer closed its call center to focus its marketing on infomercials. This timing reminded me of what Jacob thought after his dream of angels ascending and descending from a ladder to heaven: "When Jacob awoke from his sleep, he thought, 'Surely the LORD is in this place, and I was not aware of it'" (Gen. 28:16).

However, after eighteen months at the church, the youth pastor I worked with left the church for another ministry opportunity. I met with Pastor Larry and told him of my desire to take his place. Smiling, he replied, "To be a pastor in our church rather than an intern of ministry, you have to be married. If I hire a pastor for the money I am paying, I'd better get a wife included in the deal."

As a literal thinker, I missed the "two for the price of one" joke. I felt heartbroken. Because of my single status I could not be considered as a pastoral candidate.

About a month after being turned down, I attended a Tuesday night worship service at Rochester College. In the hall outside the chapel I saw a job posting from a church in a nearby city regarding a part-time associate pastor of youth ministry. I sent my résumé and got hired two weeks later. Thus, I wound up with a full-time staff position and a part-time youth pastor's post while also serving as a professor of theology at a school of ministry.

CHANCE OF A LIFETIME?

In 2003 Pastor Larry met a prominent minister whom I admired and invited him to be a guest speaker at his ministry training school. That day, after finishing his message on eschatology, the minister came over to me and we began talking. He knew that I had memorized thousands of verses and asked for some of my best preaching messages and writings. He told me to drop them off at his office. After that we could meet, and he would consider promoting me through his ministry.

Over the next few weeks I produced a special ninety-minute CD titled *The Now and Not-Yet Side of Faith*. I even hired a professional graphic designer to create the CD's cover. After much prayer I delivered these items to the minister's office. Then about a month later a ministry representative contacted me to arrange a meeting. Excited about what seemed to be my dream finally coming true, I quoted this psalm: "Will the Lord reject forever? Will he never show his favor again?" (Ps. 77:7).

The day we met (5/11/05), I told the minister that the previous day had marked my thirtieth birthday, which reminded me of the verse from Luke: "Now Jesus himself was about thirty years old when he began his ministry" (Luke 3:23).

The minister told me he had enjoyed reading my writing and hearing my messages. As he sipped black coffee, he told me he would help me in the ministry by promoting me in his ministry publication. This would enable me to receive speaking invitations from churches across the country that were connected to this man's ministry. As we were leaving, he told me I would be hearing from him soon.

Though it took more than three months, that call came. When it did, my excitement quickly faded.

"I have some sad news," the caller said. He then went on to tell me the minister did not feel peace about raising me up for ministry at that time.

As I laid down the receiver, tears gushed down my face. The director of children ministries lovingly put his hand on my shoulders and encouraged me. I appreciated that, since at that point I felt like the biblical character Job, when he said, "My face is red with weeping, dark shadows ring my eyes" (Job 16:16). Though determined to hear from God, when I prayed it seemed like heaven stood silent, as if the words of Deuteronomy 28:23 had come true: "The sky over your head will be bronze, the ground beneath you iron."

Drained of motivation and devastated by this unexpected turn of events, I prayed again as I lay down to sleep that night: "God, please speak to me, Your servant. Let me know what is standing in the way of the ministry. I will fast from food until I hear Your voice. Let Your Spirit and love direct my steps."

HOOKED ON A FEELING

Almost two weeks into this fast, a friend and I attended an event at a church in our area. After the service, as my friend socialized with some people he knew, a beautiful young woman approached me and said, "God told me to give you my number."

It was love at first sight. We met up that week, and on our first date, Jenna told me she typically worked out of town but had been home for a while due to illness. Before her conversion, she said, she had been a partier, but now she was sold out to Jesus.

Whenever I introduced her to my friends, they always

commented on how attractive she was. They'd pat me on the back and tell me how lucky I was. For the first time in my life I felt attractive and popular. I felt like I was on cloud nine; everything seemed to be perfect.

We crossed the two-month mark without a dark cloud appearing on the horizon. It felt safe to roam the friendly skies. One day, while we were at her house looking at a photo album, a letter fluttered out. Jenna pointed to the date on it and said, "This is the date the doctor told me to take time off work to fully recover. If I had been traveling, I would never have met you." I interpreted this letter as a sign from God, a burning bush not consumed, á la Exodus 3. The date was the day the previous girl I had believed was "the one" had married someone else.

However, I would learn to be wary of such happy feelings. Happiness is like the ocean waves because it's based on what happens. At any time, the feeling of happiness can change by an unexpected event. Joy is like the ocean floor, unchanging—an inner peace from God. As Kelly Langston, whose son, Alec, has autism, wrote in her book: "Joy is not simply pasting on a smile, but rather a state of being, that is the fruit of knowing and serving God. And it fills us to the brim with contentment and delight. Joy enables us to soar above autism and live the life God intended for us."[4]

Houston, We Have a Problem

As the snow covered my car, Jenna and I held hands as we talked and watched white dots descend from the pitch black sky. Gazing at me with her charming eyes, Jenna told me she believed I was the one she was to marry and suggested we look at rings.

The next afternoon I left work early. As I drove to Jenna's house, Petra's song "Don't Let Your Heart Be Hardened" came on the radio. Throughout the drive I kept repeating the lyrics to not let my heart be hardened but to keep it pure and broken before Jesus.

As I sang, my thoughts transported me to my ORU days and a girl I'll call "Marie." I met her in class one day, and after a few days I asked for her number. She said she wasn't feeling led to date anyone just then. But we continued to talk, and I held on to the hope that she might be the girl for me. I thought, somewhat naïvely, that the first girl I dated at ORU would be the one I married.

I remembered the "burning bush" experience that caused me to believe Marie was that one. The church I attended was sponsoring a college camping trip that cost fifty dollars, too high a price for a poor college student living on Ramen noodles. Yet, since Marie would be going, I felt I *had to go.* My roommate got us to the service early so we could sit front and center. Soon after I sensed God speaking life to me just as He had to Moses in the desert. It happened when a staff member announced, "Get your Bibles ready! We will give a free camping pass to the first person who reads 1 Corinthians 9:24."

I jumped on the stage in a single leap.

"Where's your Bible?" she said.

"I am a walking Bible!" I said before quoting: "Do you not know that in a race all the runners run, but only one gets the prize? Run in such a way as to get the prize." The congregation of students applauded as I was handed a free pass for the outing.

The camping weekend was a blast, and I felt sure this was God's way of giving me a sign about His plans for my future. So you can imagine my despair when she later married someone else.

When I parked in Jenna's driveway, I laughed and said to

myself, "Now Marie has married someone else, and soon I will be looking at rings."

LOOKING AT RINGS

That day, as we walked through the jewelry store, Jenna reminded me that her dream ring would have the four Cs—clarity, cut, color, and carat. Then, there was the fifth C (which all men hate): cost.

When a ring caught Jenna's attention, I asked the salesperson to take it out. But when she did, I felt a distinct lack of peace. I quickly handed the ring back to the saleswoman and said, "We'll need some more time" before rushing into the snowflake-laced, starless night.

On the way back we went to visit Jenna's parents. In her parents' driveway I held her hands, looked her in the eyes and asked, "Do you really love me? Will you remain faithful?"

Turning her eyes from me (a bad sign), she answered in a gentle voice, "I was in a relationship with my last boyfriend for several years, and I never cheated on him."

Later I began to get the impression that she wasn't being completely honest with me. People who knew her would make comments about her job that made me wonder if there were some things she wasn't telling me.

I began to experience a roller coaster of emotions, and one day when I dropped her off at her house, I turned to her and said, "Let's pray and hear what God is saying." We held hands while I prayed, but then she suddenly asked me to stop. "I feel like I'm suffocating right now," she said.

The next day we broke up. I felt dead inside and abandoned by God. Another killer whale of rejection had struck.

Round Two

A month later, when I returned from a five-mile run, my mom said, "Jenna called you and wants to see you again."

As we talked on the phone, she disclosed her fears and insecurities. This conversation led to me taking Jenna out for coffee the next night. When I stopped to pick her up, she asked me to carry some trash cans to the street. On top of one can sat a bulletin board covered with pictures of her ex-boyfriend. Looking at the board, she announced, "I am now over him."

I couldn't help but notice that her ex-boyfriend was a handsome man who wore stylish clothes. In that moment I realized that Jenna had been trying to transform me into a tame, Christian version of her old boyfriend. This was why she had tried to change my hairstyle from time to time and attempted to get me to wear different clothing.

The Holy Spirit again replayed the Petra song in my heart, reminding me once again to not let my heart get hard.

We continued going out for a few more months, but we dated sporadically. (Years later I read this reflection online that started with a quote from Socrates: "The hottest love has the coldest end." The author added: "The biggest, brightest and hottest stars are the ones which blow up in the most spectacular explosions, and leave behind a black hole, the coldest...thing in the universe."[5])

When our relationship finally reached its bitter end, Jenna told me she wasn't the girl I pictured her to be. But that didn't make the breakup any easier.

During the weeks following I withdrew from everyone and sank into depression. I had transformed into a kind of Eeyore—the gloomy, gray donkey in the famed Winnie-the-Pooh books, who liked to say things are the darkest just before they go pitch black.

Just when I threatened to sink into a bottomless pit of despair, though, I began to realize that God was protecting me. That's why I didn't have peace at the jewelry store. As legendary British preacher Charles Spurgeon once said, "When you cannot trace God's hand, you can trust His heart."[6]

I decided to pray and trust God. In my prayers God kept speaking to my heart, saying, "You have nothing; I have everything. Trust Me. I am refining you like silver and gold in the furnace." As King Solomon said, "Remove the dross from the silver, and the silversmith can produce a vessel" (Prov. 25:4). I had no idea what this refining process would entail.

Soon after this the office manager at church called me into his office to tell me we needed to talk. As I started to take a seat, he said, "Due to our church's financial hardship from Michigan's economy, we will have to let you go."

This same week the senior pastor at the other church where I worked as a youth pastor called, asking if we could meet up at a restaurant nearby. After we finished our meals, he said, "I have some bad news. We can no longer afford to have a youth pastor. We'll have to let you go."

As I departed from my full-time job, the church secretary gave me a card that had a picture of an open door and the verse from Romans 8:28: "And we know that in all things God works for the good of those who love him, who have been called according to his purpose." *Yeah, right.* In a span of less than a month I found myself alone, unemployed, living with my parents, and ineligible for unemployment since I had worked for nonprofit organizations.

ON THE ROAD AGAIN

For the next two years I suffered through unsteady employment. It included working for four months at a minimum-wage job at a skateboard shop, five months at a moving company, and the remainder at an agency serving juvenile offenders. Confused and hurt, I questioned, "Where is God? What did I do to find myself in this dark predicament?"

Yet even in the midst of this painful refining process God still opened doors for me to minister. During my stint with the moving company one of the truck drivers confided in me about his marriage problems. I was able to counsel him and pray that God would restore his marriage. A young man at the agency came to me to say, "Mr. Sandison, I heard you preach at Mt. Zion's Zero Gravity Skate Park and enjoyed your message and testimony."

Near the end of this confusing time a middle-aged woman approached me after church, handed me a piece of paper, and said, "I believe this is a message for you." It read: "God has a job for you in a field that you would never expect, and this will prepare you for the ministry." A week later I was hired by a hospital as a mental health worker. After handing me my badge and keys, a woman in the human resources department led me on a quick tour through the maze of steel doors. As the door to the adult unit slammed locked behind me, I thought, "I have a master of divinity. What am I doing working in a psych ward? In seminary I never took any classes or training for this type of work!"

MISUNDERSTANDINGS

A year after I was hired, I signed up for Clinical Pastoral Education (CPE) credits at another hospital. Yet after receiving my first CPE credit, they dropped me from the program because of my autistic quirks. The supervisor overseeing my work reprimanded me for talking too loud on my cell phone at our chaplain's office. A patient (a retired journalist) requested that I read him some of my humorous fictional psych stories.

When a nurse overheard my loud voice reading these stories and the patient laughing, she reported this to my supervisor, who again reprimanded me. The final straw that led to my termination came from missing a schedule shift because I confused 12:00 a.m. with 12:00 p.m. Neurologically my brain is unable to distinguish the difference between these two figures.

While interviewing parents of ASD children, I heard many stories about similar underemployment or lost opportunities. Jill Marzo, the mother of professional surfer Clay Marzo, told me how Clay had recently "lost his sponsorship with a major surfing company because when he met their CEO, due to his Asperger's, he failed to look the CEO in the eyes and shake his hands."[7]

MASTER DESIGN

The journey in which God led me to meet my wife and fulfill His call to the ministry included numerous dark and painful moments where I was unable to see the Master's handiwork. Well-known author A. W. Tozer once said, "It is doubtful whether God can bless a man greatly until He has hurt him deeply,"[8] but in the midst of my pain I couldn't see a smidgen of blessing.

Indeed, as the years dragged by and I kept receiving wedding invitations from college friends, it seemed like the whole world was getting married. Feeling like the only single person around, I grew weary of attending Christian singles' groups in my search for a godly wife. Then a friend discovered an easier method for meeting Christian women—online dating. After not seeing Matt for a few months at any of these singles events, I called him.

"It's amazing!" he said after explaining his absence. "I am meeting a new beautiful girl every week. Ron, you have to try online dating. The girls are not stuck up like some of the ones at the church groups!"

A week later my friend created my online profile. Less than

twenty-four hours later I had my first date with an accountant. When we met for coffee, I regaled her with my travel stories and comical tales—for three solid hours. Needless to say, my ramblings cost me a chance at a second date.

However, my friend succeeded. After a year of online dating, he met his wife. The experience helped reveal to me three simple tips for successful dating:

Be interested but not hovering.

People with autism have a tendency to become obsessive and totally focused on their desired partner. This extreme focus can help an individual be successful in college or a career, but in dating it will lead to a restraining order.

It's not you; it's them.

When I worked the afternoon shift at the hospital, I would call my friend during my breaks and ask him to check my online site inbox for new prospects and messages. One time he said, "You have a great, three-page, in-depth message from Elizabeth, a school teacher, but when you ask for her phone number, she will stop corresponding with you!"

"How do you know?"

"That's what Elizabeth did to me a year ago when I sent her a message asking for her number. It's not you; it's her. I am sure Elizabeth does that to every guy."

Sure enough, after three back-and-forth e-mails, when I asked for her number, I never heard anything more.

Another time my friend declared, "Ron, you received a number from Holly in Clarkston. It is a real number, but she'll never call you back!"

"How do you know?"

"That's what happened to me last year. Holly e-mailed me her number, and when I called, she never returned the favor. It's not you; it's her."

Again, my friend was correct.

Because of a lack of self-esteem, many people—especially those on the autism spectrum—blame themselves for the other person's actions. Guys often fail to comprehend that the way a woman treats them is how she treats everyone else. If your date cancels with you, she'll break a date with the next guy as well.

Seek first to understand.

The third tip, and most important for those on the spectrum, comes from Stephen Covey's legendary best seller *The 7 Habits of Highly Effective People:* "Seek first to understand, then to be understood."[9]

As I mentioned earlier, I love to tell stories and can become obsessive about my special interests—the Bible and psychology. While dating, I often failed to listen to others. A date with a woman who broke up with me after three months illustrates my problems back then. After I had rambled on for an hour telling her my humorous stories, I failed to take time to listen to her descriptions of an epic battle with her washing machine. Her parting words were, "You never listen to me when I talk!"

Over the next three years I mastered these three concepts. Women became my new special interest. I read hundreds of books and articles on dating and went out with more than three hundred different women in my quest for a wife. I took notes after each date to improve my relationship skills and be equipped to interpret body language. I developed my social skills and became conscious of other people's felt needs in conversations.

On 5/11/10 I met my beautiful wife, Kristen, at an upscale coffee shop. Our relationship progressed slowly but surely. After two years of dating, I proposed to her at the café where we met. God took me through an incredible journey of self-awareness and refining to bring me a wife. Kristen and I married on 12/7/12. I love the psalm that says, "And the words of the LORD are flawless, like silver purified in a crucible, like gold refined purified *seven times*" (Ps. 12:6, emphasis added). It shows that God's tough word is never His last word.

SUMMARY

As you have read, God has taken me on an amazing journey and used my experiences with autism to refine me into His image. In His Sermon on the Mount, Jesus promises that the pure in heart will see God (Matt. 5:8). I have seen God fulfill His promises to me, going well beyond what I could have imagined.

This year marks my twelfth anniversary as a professor of theology at Destiny School of Ministry. And I have spent eight years working in the mental health field. This experience has given me empathy for wounded and hurting people. As a result, I have founded a ministry called Spectrum, which brings autism awareness to churches and colleges, and empowers young adults with autism, teaching them social skills so they can gain employment and independence.

On top of that, as Kristen and I celebrate our third wedding anniversary, we joyfully anticipate the newest member of the Sandison family, our daughter, Makayla Marie, due in March 2016. Even Frishma, our cat, and Babs the rabbit are excited. As the Apostle Paul declares, "But we have this treasure in jars of clay to show that this all-surpassing power is from God and not from us" (2 Cor. 4:7).

Chapter 11

THE FUTURE OF AUTISM—FULL CIRCLE

O N 9/14/14 AT 3:15 p.m.—just fifteen minutes before the end of my shift—a rumor quickly spread among the nurses and care specialists that one nurse and one care specialist would have to work overtime. Each person hoped he or she would not get selected. Just then our supervisor entered our unit. As we made eye contact, I reflected back to the New Year's Day when I started working on this book and drew mandatory overtime.

"Ron, can I see you for a moment?"

His question spoke volumes. My first thought was not that the pending overtime would sabotage my two and a half hours of scripture memorization again. Instead, I hated the thought of not spending the evening with Kristen, since she would be sound asleep when I got home after midnight.

"Ron, I hate to do this, but we have to mandate you to work the afternoon shift," he said. "With the two new units in full swing, we don't have enough staff."

As I nodded my head, I realized that I had come full circle. Thanks to my research, dozens of interviews, and writing about autism, I had developed a new self-awareness. I could see the universe beyond my narrow special interests, setting me free from the chains of clinging to rigid patterns. This coming week I would simply reorganize my schedule to spend extra time with Kristen and make up for my missed day of memory work.

Instead of throwing an autistic, honey badger–like tantrum and risking the chance of getting fired for an unprofessional outburst, I chose to have fun with my coworkers. A nurse bought the care specialists Monster energy drinks, which made the evening more enjoyable, and we watched part of the Chiefs vs. Broncos football game. As our shift drew to a close at 11:25 p.m. and the staff herded around the time clock, I contemplated, "Should I clock out at the thirty-minute mark as I always do—or at 11:26, the same time as everyone else?"

With my hand trembling, I placed my finger on the time clock scanner at 11:26, bid everyone good-bye, and headed into the dark parking lot. I felt triumphant for following John Elder Robison's advice in his book *Be Different*: "Your own rituals are okay as long as they don't interfere with your responsibilities in daily life, or make you the subject of teasing or ridicule. Rituals become a problem whenever they prevent you from doing the stuff you're supposed to do, or when they get you in trouble."[1]

Residual Quirks

Some unseen scars of autism remain, which a trained professional would notice. An example is what happened when the hospital implemented a dress code of charcoal gray scrubs for care specialists and navy blue scrubs for nurses. For my first seven years there, every day I wore khaki or corduroy pants with a polo-style shirt. After the new dress code came into effect, I dressed in my gray scrub outfit for the first time and placed my wallet in the deep side pocket. As I left my apartment, I discovered that I was walking on my tiptoes with an awkward gait because I was not used to the way the scrubs felt.

Another example took place the week of my dad's eightieth

birthday. My parents were cleaning and fixing their house prior to a visit by my brother Steve and his family from Chicago. While I concentrated on my daily Bible memory work in the guest room, Dad decided to use an electric screwdriver to repair the master bedroom's closet door.

"Please, Dad, stop the loud noise!" I declared. "I am busy with my memory work and hope to finish by 6:00 p.m. so I will be on time for supper!"

"How can you hear the electric screwdriver?" he replied. "It makes almost no noise, and I have the door closed."

Our argument went on for fifteen minutes.

I have accepted that due to my autistic sensory issues, I will probably always have difficulties with sounds, be they electric screwdrivers, the thumping of musical bass tones, or the drone of leaf blowers. And I have similar issues with such odors as bleach, nail polish, and paint thinner. Instead of having a tantrum or meltdown, though, I can seek to inform people about my weaknesses. I don't do this angrily but through such humorous remarks as, "I'm like Superman, only my kryptonite is electronic noises and bleach. I have a few super powers. I can quote over ten thousand scriptures and run a mile in four minutes and twenty-five seconds."

Parents of ASD children get used to such eccentricities. Pastor Joni Parsley told me, "When Austin is playing video games or reading comics, Rod and I have to wait until he is finished to get his attention, or he may experience a meltdown."[2] My parents experienced many arduous struggles because of my sensory-overload meltdowns at Kmart and Kroger. By the grace of God I have largely ceased such behavior, but—as you have read earlier—I still experience occasional honey badger moments.

Through intense speech therapy I have overcome my speech impediment of mispronouncing words with the letters *th* and *l* sounds. As a sophomore in high school, I was chatting on the phone with a girl named Kim when she asked, "Why does your voice lack inflections? You sound like a Transformer." Since I had a crush on her, the question embarrassed me. This monotone is another quirk common to those with Asperger's. In interviewing others with autism, I discovered I was not the only person who sounded like a robot. Former Miss Montana Alexis Wineman was ashamed of the weird sound of her voice. It took me a while, but I have learned to accept my Transformer voice.

DAZED AND CONFUSED

Autism has caused me to be a very literal, concrete thinker. I also hate any break in my daily routines, and even worse is receiving a write-up for performance or work-related issues.

The latter is illustrated by an experience at the hospital. The human resource department maintains a strict attendance policy. When someone is sick, he must call in at least two hours before his shift starts, or it is considered an unexcused absence. One December, on the day after Christmas, I woke up an hour before my shift feeling horrible because of bronchitis. I did not want to break my iron streak of never missing a day of work. Reasoning in my concrete manner, I said, "If a nurse sends me home for being contagious, my streak will continue, and I won't receive a written warning for an unexcused absence."

So I donned my outfit and stumbled out to my car, feeling dazed throughout the five-mile drive to work. When I entered the conference room, I said to the charge nurse, "I feel like I am about to pass out; please take my temperature." After placing a thermometer in my ear, she exclaimed, "Your temp is 103! I'll call the supervisor and tell him that you need to go home immediately."

The supervisor responded, "How does a guy have a 103 temperature and still come to work?"

The answer is simple—Asperger's.

UNFILTERED

I still struggle to learn to watch what I say, a common characteristic of autism. My friend Jesse Saperstein—a best-selling author with Asperger's—once told me, "My dad told me that you need a job where you will never offend the clients by your unfiltered, inappropriate comments. So I got a job at a funeral home, where all the clients are dead."

As I mentioned previously, after finishing seminary, I went to work part-time as a telemarketer for a company that sold home security systems. On the job I became frustrated with the constant *clicks* I heard when people hung up, many right after declaring, "I already have one!" Tired and frustrated one day after eight hours of constantly hearing these clicks from 90 percent of the people I called, I thought, "I'll devise the perfect response to the next homeowner."

When the next person said, "I already have a home security system; thank you..." I quickly broke in: "Please, let me ask you a few quick questions to be sure your system is up-to-date."

"OK, but keep it short. I am busy making supper."

"Is it in a black box?

"Yeah."

"Does it have an automatic timer?"

"Yeah."

"Do you cut the blue wire but never the red and orange ones?"

"Yeah."

"You don't have a home security system, miss. You have a bomb!" I replied.

Suddenly the call center fell deathly quiet. You could hear an ant sneeze. Oops!

Despite this miscue, through working with people with autism and in a psych ward, I have learned the importance of filtering my comments. So episodes like the telemarketing bomb are past history. Understanding autism has helped me to deal with my disability. Author Michael John Carley, the author with Asperger's I mentioned previously, wrote:

> Having autism can mean having great abilities, but it can also mean never leaving the home of one's parents, never holding down a job for any extended period of time, and perhaps never enjoying a satisfying intimate relationship. Yet if these conditions were understood on a broad level, circumstances would enable most diagnosees to lead happy and productive lives.[3]

BRUTALLY HONEST

Due to Asperger's, from elementary school through college I struggled with being too honest. I was sometimes brutal.

My senior year of high school, I stood next to my locker while drinking a Coke I had brought from home. The new vice principal approached me in the hall and said, "Son, we have a new school policy of no open containers or beverages from home. You cannot drink that can of Coke. Please pour it out."

Two days later while I was talking with my friend, I saw the new vice principal drinking a can of Diet Coke as he walked with another student's mom. Furious, I walked up to him and said, "Sir, we have a new school policy—no open containers or beverages from home. I am going to have to ask you to pour out your Diet Coke since it may contain alcohol." The vice principal glared at me. His eyes narrowed, and his face flushed like a ripe tomato as he said, "Son, I'll be talking to you later."

Soon after, I received a pink pass requesting I meet immediately with the vice principal. As I entered his office, he shook my hand firmly and said, "I want to reintroduce myself to you. As you know, I am the new vice principal. I want peace. The other principals and teachers warned me that I had better be on your good side."

Life with a child who displays such traits calls for unconditional love and understanding. In my interviews and research for this book, it greatly encouraged me to hear stories of so many parents' sacrifices for their children with special needs. Take Jeff Davidson, whose son, Jon Alex, has cerebral palsy and autism. He wrote:

> The world sees a boy who cannot talk, cannot walk, and cannot function independently. I see a tapestry of God's grace, God's beauty, and God's love woven together on a human canvas....God has used my son to teach me the essence of unconditional love. God has used my son to show me how to embrace my own brokenness and accept my own vulnerabilities.[4]

JOURNEY WITH AUTISM

The stories of Mikey Brannigan and Anthony Starego are two others that beautifully demonstrate the power of parents who make unbelievable sacrifices that show their love.

Although I knew about Mikey, I learned more about him by talking with his mother, Edie. Her son is so talented that by the start of his senior year of high school in 2014, more than two hundred colleges (including most Division I schools) had reached out to him. She told me how his routines include running sixty miles a week, and the evening before every race, faithfully ordering grilled eggplant at an Italian restaurant on

Long Island. His high school performances included finishing the mile in just over four minutes and a 5K in fifteen minutes and six seconds. However, the future did not always appear so bright for Mikey, which illustrates the truth that you should never curse your circumstances, because they may be the link to your destiny.

"My son's developmental milestones were well behind those of his older brother," his mom told me. "Mikey was hyperactive, impulsive, and obsessive as a youngster. When he was three, I slept in front of his door because he was an escape artist."[5]

When Edie gave birth to her first child, Patrick, she was in labor for twenty-four hours. Her youngest son, Thomas, required sixteen hours. In a remarkable foreshadowing of the future, she delivered Mikey in just two hours. "He came running out of my womb and has never stopped running," Edie jokes. Unlike his two brothers, Mikey never crawled, but he began running at ten months.

Edie's maternal instinct sensed something was wrong when he reached twelve months of age. "I'd walk into a room, and all the chairs would be lined up across the floor," she recalled. "Mikey constantly required trips to the ER for stitches from running into walls and furniture. If Mikey wanted something, he'd point and hold his Thomas-the-Tank Engine, pressed to his nose. He was nonverbal until age four."

A specialist diagnosed Mikey with autism at eighteen months old. The specialist warned his parents that he might never function in the world and would probably have to live in a group home. Mikey required six months of intensive ABA therapy to learn how to walk beside his mother instead of running. Recalls Edie: "We lived in 'autism world.' We couldn't get out, and no one else could get in. It was very isolating."

The breakthrough came when Mikey's family watched him climbing on the jungle gym at a playground. As Mikey hung from the structure while his mom watched from a distance, he suddenly looked straight at her and called, "Help me!" Edie recalls how that stunned her: "I fell to the ground and began to cry because I knew that if he could communicate his needs—unprompted—that with situational appropriateness, he could do anything."

Mikey's dad, Kevin, decided to develop his social skills through sports. During a seminar Kevin overheard a coach named Steve Cuomo talking about an athletic program for handicapped runners called Rolling Thunder. Kevin asked, "Do you have any children with autism?" Cuomo replied, "My son has autism!" Edie says Mikey's experience with Rolling Thunder was "like the hand of God came down from the sky and shifted our lives completely. It changed everything. It gave us hope."

The first time Coach Steve saw then eight-year-old Mikey run, he exclaimed, "You didn't tell me Mikey could really run!" Kevin replied, "Well, we never thought it was a good thing." Over the next few years Mikey competed in dozens of races. At the age of twelve he ran a 10K race in thirty-eight minutes, placing twenty-second in a field of five thousand. Gradually Kevin and Edie noticed their son's thinking was clearer, his academic performance was improving, and his social interactions were growing—progress she called "a miracle."

Mikey's story is a real-life example of Paul's powerful words to the Corinthian church: "Do you not know that in a race all the runners run, but only one gets the prize? Run in such a way as to get the prize. Everyone who competes in the games goes into strict training. They do it to get a crown that will not last, but we do it to get a crown that will last forever" (1 Cor. 9:24–25).

So Amazing

In middle school I daydreamed about being like former baseball player Ricky Henderson, who holds major league records for career stolen bases, runs, unintentional walks, and lead-off home runs. I thought if I could be a superstar like him, life would be so much better. I was looking for something that would relieve me of the low self-esteem and defeatist attitude I had because of the bullying I'd experienced and my awkward social interactions.

After I finished my master of divinity and entered ministry, my dad advised: "You've accomplished so much in life. Don't tell people about your disabilities or social behavioral deficits, or you will be treated differently." He viewed autism as another "project" he could fix. That is not the case, though, as so aptly pointed out during my interview with Laura Corby, a mother with two children on the spectrum. She said, "Autism is not something that can be fixed overnight, but something you deal with. It's a journey, not an event!"[6] And as Brian King, a social worker with Asperger's, observed during another interview, "Don't assume you have to make your child with autism to be like you for him or her to be happy."[7]

Indeed, I find joy in this promise from the Psalms: "The steps of a good man are ordered by the LORD, and He delights in his way" (Ps. 37:23, NKJV). I decided to discuss how God ordered my steps, and share my personal struggles, by writing this book. I have been amazed at the divine connections God has given me with the autism community—and the opportunities for ministry. Several years ago I wrote a Christian apologetics book—*Thought, Choice, Action*—for which Dr. Ron Rhodes (president of Reasoning From the Scriptures Ministries) wrote the foreword. Dr. Rhodes counseled me to read Michael Hyatt's book *Platform: Get Noticed in a Noisy World*. When I browsed Hyatt's website for a literary agent, I contacted Les Stobbe, the first agent on his list. After I e-mailed Les my proposal, he offered me a contract.

To further my abilities, in June of 2014 I attended the Write to Publish conference at Wheaton College with my mom, an artist and illustrator. While I ate lunch with Les, my mom prayed, "God, where would You like me to sit?" Immediately, a woman a few tables away waved at her and called, "I think this seat has your name on it!" That seat was across from Kelli Ra Anderson, an author, blogger, and the mother of two sons with Asperger's. After lunch my mom exclaimed, "She's amazing; you have to meet Kelli!" I enjoyed the insightful conversations Kelli and I shared. While eating lunch, Kelli mentioned some well-known pastors who have children with Asperger's.

After the conference I discovered online a past *Charisma* magazine article about Pastor Joni Parsley's testimony of raising their autistic son, Austin. After I interviewed Pastor Joni, she e-mailed me this encouraging message:

> Rod and I have always said that we wished we could have Austin's brain for just one day so that we could better understand his unique world. Obviously, that being impossible, I sought to hear other people on the spectrum like Temple Grandin and Sean Barron and even those individuals that I personally knew. Although the aforementioned offered me some insight, it was nothing like my conversation with you.
>
> The manner with which you articulated ASD was incredible! It's the first time I could speak to someone on a personal level, and most importantly, the first Christian able to incorporate God into the matter. It felt as though the heavens opened and God allowed me to hear Austin's mind speaking—it was a very powerful moment and, I've told others, one of the top ten best

moments of my life. To see God use one obscure article
to connect us with you leaves me in complete awe!

After this correspondence Pastor Joni invited me and my
wife, Kristen, to meet their family and speak at their church
in Columbus, Ohio.

MEETING THE PARSLEY FAMILY

After we checked into the Hilton hotel and started heading
toward our room, Kristen exclaimed, "Ron, it's so amazing;
look." She pointed to the elevator's ninth-floor button, labeled
"Executive Suite." I was overwhelmed with amazement as
I gazed from our room on the executive level of the hotel.
Looking out the window, I reminisced about the journey I had
traveled. I had felt the lifelong burden of Asperger's but also
God's empowering grace.

The next day when we arrived at World Harvest Church, a
gate decorated with bronze lions slowly opened, leading us
into the guest parking area. How perfect—my special interest
as a child was animals. As I mentioned earlier, from kindergarten to sixth grade I carried a stuffed prairie dog everywhere I went. As Kristen and I entered Pastor Rod's office, my
eyes surveyed with delight his vast library of books and art
collection of North American animals.

"Ron, my wife, Joni, and I have been longing to meet Kristen
and you," Pastor Rod said as he greeted us warmly. "Your testimony of overcoming autism has richly blessed us!"

After thirty minutes of conversation we headed to the sanc-
tuary. Bright lights flashed from the stage. Cameras moved in
multiple directions as the worship team thundered the chorus
to "So Amazing." Pastor Rod's voice created a shock wave
of cheers as he read my biography and invited me to share
my testimony. I looked at the packed house, where I saw my

beautiful wife cheering loudly from the front row. I realized our amazing journey had just begun.

I am not unique. God is faithful and can use your child's disabilities for His glory too. Never put a limit on the amazing things Christ will accomplish through your child.

SMALL BEGINNINGS

Sharing my diagnosis of autism has opened doors beyond anything I ever imagined. God can use the humblest of beginnings to create a perfect ending. As the Prophet Zechariah wrote: "Do not despise these small beginnings, for the Lord rejoices to see the work begin" (Zech. 4:10, NLT).

Ray and Reylene Starego know all about such origins. Theirs began when they felt a divine call to adopt an orphan who was also a special-needs child. The moment Ray and his wife laid eyes on Anthony, they knew he was the one. Due to severe disabilities, Anthony only spoke six words and had other medical issues. One requirement for potential adoptive parents was spending small increments of time with a child to get to know him. On their second visit to the foster home, when Anthony saw Ray and Reylene enter the house, he patted the seat next to him on the sofa as if to say, "Please, come and sit with me." Ray said, "We knew right then he would be ours."[8]

The director of the foster facility thought a three-year-old with autism and other special needs was unadoptable. Naturally he felt that way about Anthony, who had been in eleven different foster homes. Smiling, Ray told him, "We know that God has a special purpose for Anthony. With a caring home and supportive community, he will fulfill his purpose."

That purpose came alive in middle school, when Ray sought to help Anthony discover a sport he could participate in and develop friendships. In 2006, at the age of twelve, Anthony watched Rutgers University's kicker Jeremy Ito hit the game-winning field goal that ruined the University of Louisville's dreams of contending for a national championship. He exclaimed, "Dad, I want to play football and be a kicker like Jeremy!"

However, since many children with autism have difficulty with close contact, bright lights, and loud noises, Ray was afraid autistic sensory issues and social awkwardness would prevent his son from playing. So the caring father counseled Anthony, "Football might not be a good fit. You don't enjoy close physical contact, and as a placekicker, you could get tackled."

Seeing that Anthony was undeterred, Ray began coaching him on the skills of placekicking. When Ray saw Anthony's kicks and noticed he could not even connect from the ten-yard line, he thought, "This is a fun activity for him, but he probably will not be playing on a competitive team." Ray recalled how it took a couple weeks before one of Anthony's kicks made it through the uprights.

In an effort to help Anthony develop as a kicker, Ray sent him to a kicking camp run by former Rutgers' placekicker Lee McDonald. Known for his booming kickoffs and a game-winning field goal that propelled his team to a 1999 upset of Syracuse on national TV, McDonald had founded Special Team Solutions. All the children at the camp that year could easily kick goals from the twenty-yard line. Ray immediately faced a dilemma: Should he have Anthony kick from the ten-yard line and be singled out or let him miss from the twenty-yard line? He decided on the latter. At first, Anthony did not connect on even one kick. Yet each day he came a little closer. At the end of camp Anthony received the Most Improved Award for his determination.

Autism and years of practice empowered Anthony to become a great kicker. "Routine and repetition is everything to Anthony," Ray told me. "His adherence to routine and repetition—three steps back, two steps over, foot planted in the exact spot every time, swinging through—leads to consistency and dulls the pressure."

After joining the football team in seventh grade, Anthony's self-esteem and perseverance increased. However, his progress did hit a few obstacles through the years. In a JV scrimmage game during his sophomore year of high school, a defender attempting to block Anthony's kick smashed his left foot, leaving him with black-and-blue marks for a month. After that, Anthony told his dad, "I'm scared." Through perseverance, though, he overcame his fear and headed back onto the field.

Anthony's high school in New Jersey had endured a nineteen-year-old playoff drought in football. Midway through Anthony's senior year he won the starting placekicker's job. In his first start he made four of four extra point tries in a thrilling 28–27 win, and the coach awarded him the game ball. On the drive home Anthony told his dad, "All my life I've been a knucklehead. But I'm not one anymore."

During the next game Anthony again claimed the starting kicker's job. The highlight of Anthony's season was his last-second, game-winning field goal against a highly favored opponent. That made national headlines and earned him a guest appearance on NBC's *Today* show with Savannah Guthrie and Matt Lauer. ESPN covered Anthony's story in its film *Kick of Hope*.

THE PERFECT ENDING

However, as Anthony entered his second senior year, which New Jersey allows children with disabilities to do so they can continue to mature and develop their social skills, he faced a new challenge. The New Jersey State Interscholastic Athletic Association (NJSIAA) ruled Anthony ineligible to compete since he had already played four consecutive years of football and turned nineteen after the cutoff date in September. The

NJSIAA decided his age would give him an unfair advantage. Attorney Gary Mayerson (a board member of Autism Speaks) and his associate, Jacqueline DeVore, battled the NJSIAA in court under the Americans with Disabilities Act. One of the earlier rulings that secured Anthony the right to compete was my 1995 case, *Sandison v. MHSAA*.

Five games into his second senior year, Anthony again won the starting kicker position. Led by a star quarterback and running back, and great defense, the team reached the pinnacle of success. Anthony continued inspiring others while making history as the first special-needs student in New Jersey history to play in a state championship game. His kick contributed two extra points toward his school's 26–15 win. He also became the first autistic player in New Jersey to achieve a postseason accolade when coaches selected him as All-Division kicker. This honor enabled him to compete in the US Army All-Shore Gridiron Classic and kick another game-winning field goal.

A strapping six-foot-four, Anthony has an IQ of 53 and only reads at a third-grade level. Yet he also possesses the heart of a champion and refuses to quit. After high school, he went on to play football at a junior college.

"He's really blossomed into a kid that makes a difference in people's lives, and he does it just by being who he is," Ray says. He encourages parents of special-needs children to not rule out anything. "What Anthony's done has already far exceeded what many expected," Ray says. "So why should anything be impossible? Never put a limit on your child."

HIDDEN BLESSINGS

During my research I received numerous e-mails and Facebook messages from parents who encouraged me to also share the stories of individuals in their twenties who are unable to speak or use the restroom without assistance.

"How is the Christian message applicable to our situation?" asked one mother. "My son is twenty-five and requires constant twenty-four-hour care and has an IQ in the low forties. We prayed for a miracle. Why has God ignored our desperate plea?"

I know how she feels. One time my supervisor assigned me to provide one-on-one care for a child with Asperger's. Midway through the shift, when another child made an inappropriate comment about the boy's mom, he experienced a meltdown. He quickly started drawing guns on the walls and throwing crayons like torpedoes. His spit connected with the charge nurse's lip, who ordered he be placed in the "quiet room" until he could calm down.

As I watched him scream, I remembered the teacher in elementary school who locked me in a room with a punching bag during a meltdown. During such episodes I felt like I was being pulled from my own skin, with every one of my sensory nerves screaming. My body would become stiff as my mind slowly went blank and I banged my head relentlessly. Reflecting on this gave me a new awareness of the stress and pain my parents experienced—and a vastly increased appreciation for all their help.

The hidden blessing of raising a child with special needs is receiving God's strength and grace to help your child while demonstrating the power of unconditional love. Your child may never be able to care for himself or herself, and yet you love your child unconditionally. The love you have for your ASD child is similar to the love God has for us. We can never earn His love or deserve it, and yet He still loves us unconditionally. You may never experience a breakthrough, or the kind of answer you hope to see, but God will strengthen you to endure.

Patty Myers, whose son Charlie has autism, encourages parents to look at the positive instead of dwelling on the negative, saying, "Focus on what they can do more than what they can't do. Find another family who is ahead of the journey you are on at least [five] years or so. It is invaluable to talk with someone else who has been through the same trials and who has prevailed or who has advice on how to approach this. I am grateful each day for the journey we are on, even on the toughest of days. I know God is using my Charlie to teach me so much more about Christ."[9]

We may never be able to answer the "why" questions, such as, "Why did God allow my child to have autism?" Or, "Why was I born with Asperger's?" One of the early church fathers, St. Athanasius—who played a pivotal role in the formation of the New Testament canon and the development of the theology of the Trinity—wrote a short book, *The Life of St. Anthony the Great*. St. Athanasius shares the story from the fourth century of two men near death's door who went on a journey of faith into a desert in Egypt to seek the monk St. Anthony so he could heal them. On their quest for healing, they both became disoriented and lost. St. Anthony prayed and received a vision from God of one man lying dead and his soul being carried to heaven; in the vision, the other man was about to die. He quickly sent two of his servants with water to rescue the man. When St. Anthony laid hands on the man, he was instantly healed by Christ.

St. Athanasius asks the readers, "Why did God allow the one man to receive his healing and the other to die alone in the desert? Did the one man have more faith then the other? No, both men had equal faith, as demonstrated by their entering the desert in search of healing. God being all-powerful and all-knowing could have given St. Anthony the vision a day earlier so both men would survive." St. Athanasius concludes, "There is a divine mystery of healing."[10]

To this observation I would add these words from Deuteronomy 29:29: "The secret things belong to the Lord our God." God may have answered your prayers in the desert by healing your son and empowering him to speak and attend college. You may feel abandoned in the desert sandstorms as you pray daily for strength to endure your child's frequent meltdowns, with no signs of improvement. Your child, like the son of the mom who e-mailed me, might never speak on earth. Yet as believers, we still have hope. When Christ returns, the nonverbal child will speak, and every physical disability will be healed. And He will wipe every tear from your eyes. On your journey, enjoy the hidden blessings from God, and never lose hope. As Kristine Barnett encourages parents, "Look for the spark in your child, and develop his or her gifts."

Summary

As we have discovered throughout this book, children with autism can achieve amazing things when they receive love and support. Never allow the label of autism to limit your child's potential. As Luke 1:37 states, "For with God nothing will be impossible" (mev). Focus on your child's interests and encourage their gifts to help them gain independence. In time, your child's life will become a testimony of the love and grace of God. As Psalm 145:4 says, "Generation after generation stands in awe of your work; each one tells stories of your mighty acts" (The Message).

UNDERSTANDING AUTISM

LABELS AND THE ASD DIAGNOSIS

P ARENTS FEAR RECEIVING the news that their child is being diagnosed with autism spectrum disorder (ASD), often because of the stigma and labels attached to it. But there are both advantages and disadvantages to labeling children with ASD.

Advantages of labeling

1. Receive special education

2. Eligible to receive more help in the classroom

3. Special programs that can help your child

4. Can qualify for government services to help your child

5. Founding of research programs

Disadvantages of labeling

1. Stigmatize the child and cause peers to treat them differently

2. May cause the child to feel denied from certain opportunities

3. Focuses only on what the child cannot do rather than what they can

4. May have negative effect on child's self-esteem and self-image

5. May cause the parents to have lower expectations for their child

THE INCREASED PREVALENCE OF AUTISM

Statistics show a dramatic rise in the prevalence of autism since the 1980s—up as much as 600 percent. It is not clear what is causing this increase, but Simon Baron-Cohen has developed the following theory:

1. **There has been a shift from categorical to spectrum view of autism**. Now that we recognize shades of autism, we can include not just the extreme cases but also the milder cases.

2. **We have better recognition, better training, and better services**. Now that most primary health professionals (e.g., speech therapists, general practitioners, health visitors, child psychologists, child psychiatrists, and pediatricians) are taught about the autistic spectrum and there are clinics to assess it in every small town—not just major metropolitan areas—clinics are seeing more children for assessments.

3. **The autism spectrum now includes new subgroups**. In the old days, only classic autism was recognized, but now children and adults with different forms of autism spectrum conditions (i.e., Asperger's syndrome, atypical autism, PDD-NOS) are included.[1]

THE PICTURE EXCHANGE
COMMUNICATION SYSTEM (PECS)

The Picture Exchange Communication System (PECS) begins by teaching an individual to give a picture of a desired item to a "communicative partner," who immediately honors the exchange as a request. The system goes on to teach discrimination of pictures and how to put them together in sentences. In the more advanced phases, individuals are taught to answer questions and to comment.[2] There are six phases of PECS:[3]

- **Phase 1: How to Communicate**
  The child with autism learns to exchange single pictures for items or activities they really want.

- **Phase 2: Distance and Persistence**
  Still using single pictures, the child with autism learns to generalize this new skill by using it in different places, with different people, and across distances. The child is also taught to be a more persistent communicator.

- **Phase 3: Discrimination Between Symbols**
  The child with autism learns to select from two or more pictures to ask for his or her favorite things. These are placed in a communication book, typically a three-ring binder with Velcro strips where pictures can be stored and easily removed for communication.

- **Phase 4: Using Phrases**
  The child with autism learns to construct simple sentences on a detachable sentence strip using an "I want" picture followed by a picture of the item being requested.

- **Phase 5: Answering a Direct Question**
  The child with autism learns to use PECS to answer the question, "What do you want?"

- **Phase 6: Commenting**
  Now the child with autism is taught to comment in response to questions such as, "What do you see?", "What do you hear?", and "What is it?" They learn to make up sentences starting with I see, I hear, I feel, It is a…, etc.

TEN IMPORTANT FACTS ABOUT BULLYING

1. Students with disabilities are more likely to be bullied than nondisabled peers.

2. Bullying affects a student's ability to learn.

3. Bullying based on a student's disability may be considered harassment.

4. Under federal laws disability harassment is a civil rights violation.

5. Under state laws students have a legal right not to be targeted for bullying.

6. Adult response to bullying is important and can help prevent it.

7. Parents and other concerned adults must learn all the resources available to help prevent bullying.

8. Bystanders have power; more than 50 percent of bullying stops when a peer intervenes.

9. Parents must teach their children the importance of self-advocacy.

10. Parents must let the bullied child know he or she is not alone and has support.

REPORTING AN ADA COMPLAINT

T O FILE A complaint reporting a violation of the Americans with Disabilities Act, write to:

US Department of Justice
950 Pennsylvania Avenue, NW
Civil Rights Division
Disability Rights Section – 1425 NYAV
Washington, DC 20530

To file an ADA complaint by fax, contact (202) 307-1197.

To file an ADA complaint by e-mail, write to ADA .complaint@usdoj.gov.

No matter which option you choose, keep a copy of your complaint and original supporting documents for your records.

For more information about ADA compliance, visit http:// www.ada.gov/filing_complaint.htm.

BIBLICAL PRINCIPLES FOR ADVOCACY

L UKE, A FIRST-CENTURY follower of Christ, was a physician who wrote two books in the New Testament. His writings included an emphasis on the importance of advocating for the poor, outcasts, and innocent (Luke 1:53–54; 4:18–19).

The Gospel of Luke and the Book of Acts are apologetics that advocate for Christ and His followers, showing they were innocent of any crimes against Rome. In Luke's Gospel, when Jesus died on the cross, the centurion worshipped God, saying, "Surely this man was innocent" (Luke 23:47, NLT). The bystanders who witnessed Christ's crucifixion beat their breasts to display their sorrow at the death of an innocent man.

One of the criminals crucified with Christ mocked Jesus. In response, the other criminal rebuked him: "'Don't you fear God,' he said, 'since you are under the same sentence? We are punished justly, for we are getting what our deeds deserve. But this man has done nothing wrong'" (Luke 23:40–41).

When Stephen was brought before the Sanhedrin, Luke records, "His face was like the face of an angel" (Acts 6:15). Luke also wrote that while Paul was awaiting trial before Caesar, he declared to the Jewish leaders, "I have done nothing against our people…I was arrested in Jerusalem and handed over to the Romans. They examined me and wanted to release me, because I was not guilty of any crime" (Acts 28:17–18).

Luke's writings contain four key principles for acting as an advocate. They are essential for every parent of a special-needs child.

DEFEND THE HELPLESS

The weakest voice deserves the greatest defense. The parable of the good Samaritan (Luke 10:25–37) beautifully illustrates this truth. In this story Jesus describes how the religious leaders failed to obey the ancient oral law mandating the preservation of life. The preservation of life takes precedence over ceremonial laws, meaning we should do whatever is necessary to save someone in need. The priest and Levite who saw the injured man ignored his desperate cry for fear of becoming ceremonially unclean. However, moved by compassion, the Samaritan helped the man, who had been the victim of robbers, by bandaging his wounds and taking him to an inn.

USE EVERY AVAILABLE RESOURCE

Jesus taught the principle of stewardship in His parable about a shrewd manager (Luke 16:1–9). In the story, a master accused his manager of wasting his possessions. Fearing the loss of employment, the manager advocated for his cause by winning the favor of his master's debtors by lowering the amount they owed his master. He knew they would appreciate his gesture and welcome him into their homes when he wound up on the street. Jesus concluded this parable: "The master commended the dishonest manager because he had acted shrewdly. For the people of this world are more shrewd in dealing with their own kind than are the people of the light. I tell you, use worldly wealth to gain friends for yourselves, so that when it is gone, you will be welcomed into eternal dwellings" (vv. 8–9).

The community of the Essenes at Qumran—who wrote the Dead Sea Scrolls—lived in isolation, dwelling in caves and having limited contact with the outside world. They referred to their isolated community as the "people of light." Their leaders forbade the community from using any Roman coins containing engraved images. Unlike the community of Qumran, an advocate maintains a far-ranging group of contacts in an effort to employ every resource necessary for his or her child's cause. Networking is essential because there is power and strength in numbers. As wise Solomon wrote: "A *cord of three strands* is *not quickly broken*" (Eccles. 4:12, emphasis added).

USE TENACITY AND BOLDNESS

Jesus taught the principle of tenacity in His parable about an unjust judge (Luke 18:1–8). Luke records how Jesus used the story to teach His disciples to always pray and never give up. In the parable, a widow advocating for justice wouldn't accept the judge's refusal. She demonstrated her *chutzpah* by refusing to back down. Brad Young, a professor of biblical literature at Oral Roberts University and an expert in Hebrew and Greek, defines *chutzpah* as "headstrong persistence, brazen impudence, unyielding tenacity, bold determination, and raw nerve."[1] Such persistence worked. Realizing this widow would continue to demand justice, the judge finally yielded to her request for the sole purpose of silencing her cry.

PLACE YOUR CHILD'S CAUSE IN GOD'S HANDS

Luke teaches the principle of trust in his narrative about Stephen's martyrdom (Acts 7:54–59). Outraged at Stephen's message about their stiff-necked behavior and that of their ancestors, the Jewish leaders dragged him outside the city and stoned him. As the stones crashed against him, Stephen prayed, "Lord Jesus, receive my spirit.…Lord, do not hold this sin against them" (vv. 59–60). Here it is worth noting that at the beginning of Acts 8, Luke comments that Saul gave his approval to this killing.

Only in this passage of Scripture is Jesus depicted as standing at the right hand of God rather than sitting. Jesus's standing at the right hand of God demonstrates that God advocated for Stephen's cause and would bring justice. Jesus brought this justice by transforming Stephen's leading persecutor, Saul, into the Apostle Paul, a premier evangelist and the most prolific writer of the New Testament.

We too can receive justice as we trust God and follow these biblical principles of advocacy.

BIBLIOGRAPHY

Anderson, Brent and Linda Gund Anderson. *Unintentional Humor: Celebrating the Literal Mind of Autism*. Np: Gund Publishing, 2011.

Attwood, Tony. *The Complete Guide to Asperger's Syndrome*. Philadelphia, PA: Jessica Kingsley Publishers, 2007.

Attwood, Tony, Craig R. Evans, and Anita Lesko. *Been There. Done That. Try This!: An Aspie's Guide to Life on Earth*. Philadelphia, PA: Jessica Kingsley Publishers, 2014.

Aune, Beth. *Behavior Solutions for the Home and Community*. Arlington, TX: Future Horizons, 2014.

Baron-Cohen, Simon. *Autism and Asperger Syndrome: The Facts*. Oxford: Oxford University Press, 2008.

———. *Mindblindness: An Essay on Autism and Theory of Mind*. Cambridge, MA: MIT Press, 1997.

———. *The Science of Evil: On Empathy and the Origins of Cruelty*. New York: Basic Books, 2011.

Barron, Judy and Sean Barron. *There's a Boy in Here: Emerging From the Bonds of Autism*. Arlington, TX: Future Horizons, 2002.

Barnett, Kristine. *The Spark: A Mother's Story of Nurturing Genius*. New York: Random House, 2013.

Biklen, Douglas. *Autism and Myth of the Person Alone*. New York: New York University Press, 2005.

Bissonnette, Barbara. *The Complete Guide to Getting a Job for People With Asperger's Syndrome: Find the Right Career and Get Hired.* Philadelphia, PA: Jessica Kingsley Publishers, 2013.

Bolduc, Kathleen Deyer. *His Name Is Joel: Searching for God in a Son's Disability.* Louisville, KY: Bridge Resources, 1999.

Brown, Stuart with Christopher Vaughan. *Play.* New York: Penguin Group, 2009.

Carley, Michael J. *Asperger's From the Inside Out.* New York: Perigee Books, 2008.

Chambers, Oswald. *My Utmost for His Highest.* Uhrichsville, OH: Barbour Publishing, 1935.

Cline, Foster and Jim Fay. *Parenting With Love and Logic.* Colorado Springs, CO: NavPress, 2006.

Covey, Stephen R. *The 7 Habits of Highly Effective People.* New York: Simon & Schuster, 1989.

Colson, Emily. *Dancing With Max.* Grand Rapids, MI: Zondervan, 2010.

Crawford, Brad, and Alisha Crawford. *The First Steps: A Parent's Guide to Fighting Autism.* Maitland, FL: Xulon Press, 2010.

Devananda, Angelo. *Total Surrender: Mother Teresa.* Ann Arbor, MI: Servant Publications, 1985.

Fowler, Melanie. *Look at My Eyes: Autism Spectrum Disorders: Autism and PDD-NOS.* Dallas, TX: Brown Christian Press, 2011.

Gillibrand, John. *Disabled Church—Disabled Society.* Philadelphia, PA: Jessica Kingsley Publishers, 2010.

Grandin, Temple. *Thinking in Pictures and Other Reports From My Life With Autism*. New York: Vintage Books, 1995.

———. *The Way I See It: A Personal Look at Autism & Asperger's*. Arlington, TX: Future Horizons, 2011.

Grandin, Temple and Margaret M. Scariano. *Emergence: Labeled Autistic*. New York: Warner Books, 1996.

Grandin, Temple and Richard Panek. *The Autistic Brain: Thinking Across the Spectrum*. New York: Houghton Mifflin Harcourt, 2013.

Hamilton, Lynn M. *Facing Autism: Giving Parents Reasons for Hope and Guidance for Help*. Colorado Springs, CO: WaterBrook Press, 2000.

Hendrickson, Laura. *Finding Your Child's Way on the Autism Spectrum*. Chicago, IL: Moody Publishers, 2009.

Kearney, Albert J. *Understanding Applied Behavior Analysis: An Introduction to ABA for Parents, Teachers, and Other Professionals*. Philadelphia, PA: Jessica Kingsley Publishers, 2008.

Hodgdon, Linda A. *Solving Behavior Problems in Autism*. Troy, MI: QuirkRoberts Publishing, 1999.

Keenan, Mickey, Ken P. Kerr, and Karola Dillenburger. *Parents' Education as Autism Therapists: Applied Behaviour Analysis in Context*. Philadelphia, PA: Jessica Kingsley Publishers, 2000.

Keenan, Mickey, Mary Henderson, Ken P. Kerr, and Karola Dillenburger. *Applied Behaviour Analysis and Autism*. Philadelphia, PA: Jessica Kingsley Publishers, 2006.

King, Brian R. *Strategies for Building Successful Relationships With People on the Autism Spectrum*. Philadelphia, PA: Jessica Kingsley Publishers, 2012.

Koegel, Lynn Kern and Claire LaZebnik. *Overcoming Autism*. New York: Viking, 2004.

Labosh, Kathy and LaNita Miller. *The Child With Autism at Home and in the Community*. Arlington, TX: Future Horizons, 2011.

Langston, Kelly. *Autism's Hidden Blessings*. Grand Rapids, MI: Kregel Publications, 2009.

Lawson, Wendy. *Understanding and Working With the Spectrum of Autism: An Insider's View*. Philadelphia, PA: Jessica Kingsley Publishers, 2001.

Lovaas, Ivar O. *Teaching Developmentally Disabled Children: The Me Book*. Austin, TX: PRO-ED, 1981.

Maurice, Catherine. *Let Me Hear Your Voice: A Family's Triumph Over Autism*. New York: Alfred Knopf, 1993.

Newman, Barbara J. *Autism and Your Church*. Grand Rapids, MI: Friendship Ministries, 2011.

Oates, Wayne E. *The Presence of God in Pastoral Counseling*. Np: Word Books, 1986.

Newman, Bobby. *When Everybody Cares: Case Studies of ABA With People With Autism*. New York: AMAC, 1999.

Peek, Fran with Lisa L. Hanson. *The Life and Message of the Real Rain Man: the Journey of a Mega-Savant*. Port Chester, NY: Dude Publishing, 2008.

Powers, Michael D. with Janet Poland. *Asperger Syndrome & Your Child: A Parent's Guide*. New York: Harper Collins, 2002.

Robison, John Elder. *Be Different: My Adventures With Asperger's and My Advice for Fellow Aspergians, Misfits, Families, and Teachers*. New York: Broadway Paperbacks, 2011.

———. *Look Me in the Eye: My Life With Asperger's.* New York: Three Rivers Press, 2007.

Rudy, Lisa Jo. *Get Out, Explore, and Have Fun!.* Philadelphia, PA: Jessica Kingsley Publishers, 2010.

Sainsbury, Clare. 2000. *Martian in the Playground.* Bristol, UK: Lucky Duck Publishing, 2000.

Saperstein, Jesse A. *Atypical: Life With Asperger's in 20⅓ Chapters.* New York: Perigee Books, 2010.

———. *Getting a Life With Asperger's.* New York: Perigee Books, 2014.

Simmons, Karen L. and Bill Davis. *Autism Tomorrow: The Complete Guide to Help Your Child Thrive in the Real World.* Seattle, WA: Exceptional Resources, Inc, 2010.

Simmons, Lisa. *I Would Have Said Yes: A Family's Journey with Autism.* Bloomington, IN: WestBow Press, 2012.

Simone, Rudy. *Asperger's on the Job: Must-Have Advice for People With Asperger's or High Functioning Autism, and Their Employers, Educators, and Advocates.* Arlington, TX: Future Horizons, 2010.

Stillman, William. *The Autism Answer Book.* Naperville, IL: Sourcebooks, Inc., 2007.

———. *Autism and the God Connection.* Naperville, IL: Sourcebooks, Inc., 2006.

———. *Empowered Autism Parenting.* San Francisco: Jossey-Bass, 2009.

———. *The Soul of Autism.* Franklin Lakes, NJ: New Page Books, 2008.

Volkmar, Fred R. and Lisa A. Wiesner. *A Practical Guide to Autism.* Hoboken, NJ: John Wiley & Sons, Inc., 2009.

Willey, Liane Holliday. *Pretending to be Normal: Living With Asperger's Syndrome*. Philadelphia, PA: Jessica Kingsley Publishers, 1999.

Yong, Amos. *The Bible, Disability, and the Church*. Grand Rapids, MI: William B. Eerdmans, 2011.

Young, Lynda T. *Hope for Families of Children on the Spectrum*. Abilene, TX: Leaf Wood Publishers, 2011.

NOTES

CHAPTER 1—UNDERSTANDING AUTISM

1. Goodreads, "Charles H. Spurgeon Quotes," accessed December 15, 2015, http://www.goodreads.com/quotes/44599-by-perseverance-the-snail-reached-the-ark.

2. Michael D. Powers with Janet Poland, *Asperger Syndrome & Your Child: A Parent's Guide* (New York: HarperCollins, 2002), 225.

3. The author interviewed more than forty experts and authors in the autism community and more than forty parents of children with autism.

4. Centers for Disease Control and Prevention, "Autism Spectrum Disorder (ASD)," accessed December 15, 2015, http://www.cdc.gov/ncbddd/autism/data.html.

5. Simon Baron-Cohen, *Autism and Asperger Syndrome: The Facts* (Oxford, England: Oxford University Press, 2008), 25.

6. "About Autism," Autism Society, accessed December 15, 2015, http://www.autism-society.org/about-autism.

7. William Stillman, *Autism Answer Book* (Naperville, IL: Sourcebooks Inc., 2007), 2.

8. W. L. Heward, "Characteristics of Children With Autism Spectrum Disorders," Education.com, July 20, 2010, accessed October 29, 2015, http://www.education.com/reference/article/children-autism-spectrum-disorders/.

9. Lynda T. Young, *Hope for Families of Children on the Autistic Spectrum* (Abilene, TX: Leafwood Publishers, 2011), 21.

10. Lisa Jo Rudy, "What Are the Different Names of Autism Spectrum Disorder?" July 22, 2015, accessed October 29, 2015, http://autism.about.com/od/whatisautism/tp/ASDs.htm.

11. Kate Miller-Wilson, "Different Levels of Autism," accessed October 29, 2015, http://autism.lovetoknow.com/Different_Levels_of_Autism.

12. Temple Grandin and Richard Panek, *The Autistic Brain: Thinking Across the Spectrum* (New York: Houghton Mifflin Harcourt, 2013), 119.

13. William Stillman, *The Soul of Autism* (Franklin Lakes, NJ: New Page Books, 2008), 52.

14. Baron-Cohen, *Autism and Asperger Syndrome*, 37.

15. Tony Attwood, *The Complete Guide to Asperger's Syndrome* (Philadelphia, PA: Jessica Kingsley Publishers, 2007), 53.

16. Melanie Fowler, *Look at My Eyes* (Dallas, TX: Brown Christian Press, 2011), 13.

17. H. J. Larson et al., "Risk Factors for Autism: Perinatal Factors, Parental Psychiatric History, and Socioeconomic Status." *American Journal of Epidemiology* 161, no. 10 (May 15, 2005): 916–995, http://www.ncbi.nlm.nih.gov/pubmed/15870155.

18. Daniel J. DeNoon, "Autism Risk Rises With Mother's Age," *Autism Spectrum Disorder Health Center*, February 8, 2010, accessed December 15, 2015, http://www.webmd.com/brain/autism/news/20100208/autism-risk-rises-with-mothers-age.

19. Caroline DiBattisto, "Autism Spectrum Disorder: Pathogenesis and Pathophysiology," MedMerits, http://www.medmerits.com/index.php/article/autistic_disorders/P5.

20. Margaret L. Bauman, "Microscopic Neuroanatomic Abnormalities in Autism," *Pediatrics* 87, no. 5 (May 1, 1991): 791–796, http://pediatrics.aappublications.org/content/87/5/791.

21. Powers, *Asperger Syndrome & Your Child*, 31.

22. Peter Jenson, "How Early Can a Child Be Diagnosed With Autism?" *Chicago Tribune*, May 15, 2013, accessed October 29, 2015, http://articles.chicagotribune.com/2013-05-15/health/sc-health-0515-child-health-autism-20130515_1_autism-social-interaction-and-behavior-young-child.

23. Ibid.

24. Stephen Mark Shore, in communication with the author, August 18, 2014. Used with permission.

25. Toby Evans, in communication with the author. Used with permission.

26. Powers, *Asperger Syndrome & Your Child*, 22–23.

CHAPTER 2—INSIDERS' PERSPECTIVES

1. Karen Trinkkaus, "The Problems With Giving Your Bird a Mirror," FeistyFeathers.com, accessed October 29, 2015, http://feistyhome.phpwebhosting.com/mirrors.htm.

2. Simon Baron-Cohen, *The Science of Evil: On Empathy and the Origins of Cruelty* (New York: Basic Books, 2011), 95–96.

3. Blake Eastman, "How Much of Communication Is Really Non-verbal?" The Nonverbal Group, accessed October 29, 2015, http://www.nonverbalgroup.com/2011/08/how-much-of-communication-is-really-nonverbal.

4. Laura Hendrickson, *Finding Your Child's Way on the Autism Spectrum* (Chicago: Moody Publishers, 2009), 81.

5. The Autism Community Store can be found at https://www.autismcommunitystore.com.

6. Powers, *Asperger Syndrome & Your Child*, 124.

7. Carol Gray Social Stories, http://carolgraysocialstories.com/social-stories/.

8. Melanie Fowler, *Look at My Eyes* (Dallas, TX: Brown Christian Press, 2011), 54.

9. Lynn M. Hamilton, *Facing Autism* (Colorado Springs, CO: WaterBrook Press, 2000), 43.

10. Robin Hansen, "Autism Meltdowns versus Temper Tantrums," Special Education Examiner, July 11, 2009, accessed September 3, 2015, http://m.cafemom.com/groups/read_topic.php?group_id=112775&topic_id=15240104 on.

11. Gary G. Porter, "The Literal Mind of Autism," *Autism Key*, July 20, 2011, accessed December 15, 2015, http://www.autismkey.com/the-literal-mind-of-autism/.

12. Temple Grandin, *The Way I See It: A Personal Look at Autism & Asperger's* (Arlington, TX: Future Horizons, 2011), 104.

13. Powers, *Asperger Syndrome & Your Child*, 71.

14. Stillman, *Autism Answer Book*, 66.

15. Temple Grandin, *Thinking in Pictures and Other Reports From My Life With Autism* (New York: Vintage Books, 1996), 67.

16. Attwood, *The Complete Guild to Asperger's Syndrome*, 290.

17. Hamilton, *Facing Autism*, 219.

18. Grandin, *The Way I See It*, 83.

19. Lisa Jo Rudy, "What Is Stimming and Why Is It Common in Autistic People?", Autism, About.com, October 15, 2009, http://autism.about.com/od/autismterms/f/stimming.htm.

20. Lynn Kern Koegel and Claire LaZebnik, *Overcoming Autism* (New York: Viking, 2004), 114–115.

21. Grandin, *The Way I See It*, 2.

22. John Elder Robison, *Look Me in the Eye: My Life With Asperger's* (New York: Three Rivers Press, 2007), 208.

23. Hamilton, *Facing Autism*, 310.

Chapter 3—Parenting Perseverance

1. Ron Sandison, "A Mom's Advocacy for Her Son," Not Alone, August 8, 2014, accessed January 26, 2016, specialneedsparenting.net /moms-advocacy-son-guest-post. Used with permission.

2. Internet Movie Data Base, *Chariots of Fire*, "Quotes," accessed December 15, 2015, http://www.imdb.com/title/tt0082158/quotes.

3. Kristine Barnett, *The Spark: A Mother's Story of Nurturing Genius* (New York: Random House, 2013), 102.

4. Grandin and Panek, *The Autistic Brain: Thinking Across the Spectrum*, 187.

5. From author's interview with Rhonda Gelstein on August 4, 2014. You can find more of her thoughts at http://herustyglider .blogspot.com.

6. Barnett, *The Spark*, 71.

7. Ibid., 205.

8. From author's interview with Dr. Joanne Ruthsatz on April 29, 2014.

9. Ohio State University, "Link Found Between Child Prodigies and Autism," press release, November 9, 2012, accessed January 26, 2016, researchnews.osu.edu/archivechldprod.htm.

10. Christie Nicholson, "Q & A: Psychologist Joanne Ruthsatz on the Common Trait of All Prodigies," *Smart Plant*, issue 15, May 30, 2013, accessed October 15, 2015, http://www.zdnet.com/article/qa -psychologist-joanne-ruthsatz-on-the-common-trait-of-all-prodigies/.

11. Barnett, *The Spark*, 249.

12. Fred R. Volkmar and Lisa A. Wisner, *A Practical Guide to Autism* (Hoboken, NJ: John Wiley & Sons, Inc., 2009), 195.

13. Clare Sainsbury, *Martian in the Playground* (Bristol, UK: Lucky Duck Publishing, 2000), 25.

14. Laura McCarley, *Welcome to No Man's Valley* (New York: Random House, 1981); see http://www.imdb.com/title/tt0344123/.

15. Hendrickson, *Finding Your Child's Way on the Autism Spectrum*, 37.

16. Stuart Brown with Christopher Vaughan, *Play* (New York: Penguin Group, 2009), 118.

17. Lisa Jo Rudy, *Get Out, Explore, and Have Fun!* (Philadelphia: Jessica Kingsley Publishers, 2010), 21, 24.

18. Deborah Marrie, "Locked in Their Own World," *Charisma*, June 30, 2004, accessed December 15, 2015, http://www.charismamag .com/blogs/348-j15/features/healing-for-families/1263-locked-in-their -own-world.

19. Kelly Langston, "Why Did God Give Me a Child With a Special Need?", Not Alone, April 23, 2013, accessed November 3, 2015, http://specialneedsparenting.net/why-did-god-give-me-a-child-with-special-needs/.

20. Poem written by April Vernon, used by permission. See more of April's thoughts at http://secondtimearound-vernyvern.blogspot.com/.

CHAPTER 4—MENTORING

1. Temple Grandin and Margaret M. Scariano, *Emergence: Labeled Autistic* (New York: Warner Books, 1996), 82, 99–100.

2. From author's interview with Susan Osborne on August 9, 2014.

3. D. L. Moody, as quoted in "The Bible Was Not Given to Increase Our Knowledge But to Change Our Lives," Navigators, Oct. 1, 2014, emphasis added, accessed October 30, 2015, http://www.navigators.org/Tools/Newsletters/Featured%20Newsletters/Disciple/Oct%202014/Oct%202014/The%20Bible%20Was%20Not%20Given%20to%20Increase%20Our%20Knowledge.

4. From author's interview with Julie Ann Reed on May 12, 2014.

5. Some details have been changed to protect the blogger's privacy.

6. Koegel and LaZebnik, *Overcoming Autism*, 157.

7. Hendrickson, *Finding Your Child's Way on the Autism Spectrum*, 71.

8. From author's interview with Brian R. King on June 6, 2014.

CHAPTER 5—BULLY PROOFING

1. Tony Attwood, Craig R. Evans, and Anita Lesko, *Been There. Done That. Try This!: An Aspie's Guide to Life on Earth* (Philadelphia, PA: Jessica Kingsley Publishers, 2014), 253.

2. Attwood, *The Complete Guide to Asperger's Syndrome*, 95.

3. Attwood, Evans, and Lesko, *Been There. Done That. Try This!: An Aspie's Guide to Life on Earth*, 248.

4. Michael Ko, "14 Signs That Your Child Is Being Bullied or Is a Bully," *Health & Fitness,* MSN.com, February 7, 2015, accessed December 15, 2015, http://www.msn.com/en-au/health/wellness/14-signs-that-your-child-is-being-bullied-or-is-a-bully/ss-AA8Ksct.

5. Karen L. Simmons and Bill Davis, *Autism Tomorrow: The Complete Guide to Help Your Child Thrive in the Real World* (Seattle: Exceptional Resources, Inc., 2010), 121.

6. Michael John Carley, *Asperger's From the Inside Out* (New York: Perigee Books, 2008), 91.

7. Katie Celis, in a Facebook post dated April 21, 2014, accessed October 30, 2015, https://www.facebook.com/ellentv/posts/1015242 1555857240.

8. Foster Cline and Jim Fay, *Parenting With Love and Logic* (Colorado Springs, CO: NavPress, 2006), 130.

9. Kathy Labosh and LaNita Miller, *The Child With Autism at Home and in the Community* (Arlington, TX: Future Horizons, 2011), 75.

10. Grandin, *The Way I See It*, 150.

11. Frank DeFrank, "Ex-MSU Hoops Player Talks About Overcoming Autism, Bullies," *Macomb Daily*, February 24, 2014, accessed October 30, 2015, www.macombdaily.com/social-affairs/20140224 /ex-msu-hoops-player-talks-about-overcoming-autism-bullies.

12. From author's interview with Anthony Ianni on September 29, 2014.

13. Ibid.

CHAPTER 6—REDEFINING YOUR CHILD'S SELF-ESTEEM

1. Judy Barron and Sean Barron, *There's a Boy in Here: Emerging from the Bonds of Autism* (Arlington, TX: Future Horizons, 2002), 161.

2. Karen L. Simmons, "Building Self-Esteem in Children With Autism and Asperger Syndrome," Autism Today, accessed December 15, 2015, http://www.autismtoday.com/library-back/buildingself esteem.html.

3. As quoted by Jae Song, in "13 Tips to Building Self-Esteem," ThinkSimpleNow.com, accessed October 30, 2015, http:// thinksimplenow.com/happiness/the-art-of-building-self-esteem/.

4. Valerie L. Gaus, *Living Well on the Spectrum* (New York: Guilford Press, 2011), 90.

5. Attwood, Evans, and Lesko, *Been There. Done That. Try This! An Aspie's Guide to Life on Earth*, 199.

6. Ibid., 39.

7. From author's interview with Mark Youngkin on December 18, 2014.

8. Wendy Lawson, *Understanding and Working With the Spectrum of Autism: An Insider's View* (Philadelphia, PA: Jessica Kingsley Publishers, 2001, 118-119.

9. Alexis Wineman, "Alexis Wineman on Her Journey With Autism and Meeting Her Hero, Dr. Temple Grandin," FutureHorizons .com, July 11, 2014, accessed October 30, 2015, http://fhautism.com

/alexis-wineman-on-her-journey-with-autism-and-meeting-her-hero
-dr.-temple-grandin.html.

10. Tom Howard, "Miss Montana Overcame Many Challenges On
Her Way to the Crown," *Billings Gazette*, August 2, 2012, accessed
October 30, 2015, http://billingsgazette.com/news/local/miss-montana
-overcame-many-challenges-on-her-way-to-the/article_a1c54d0d-7c75
-5952-b1fd-95abb154efe9.html.

11. Information and comments about Alexis Wineman came
from the author's interview with her mother, Kimberley Butterworth
Wineman, on January 5, 2015.

12. Ibid.

13. Ibid.

14. Alexis Wineman, "Miss Montana: Autism Doesn't Define Me,"
CNN.com, January 17, 2013, accessed October 30, 2015, http://www
.cnn.com/2013/01/17/health/wineman-autism/.

15. Information and comments about Alexis Wineman came
from the author's interview with her mother, Kimberley Butterworth
Wineman, on January 5, 2015. Alexis made similar comments in
a Miss Montana promotional video, which can be viewed at http://
zap2it.com/2013/01/miss-america-2013-miss-montana-alexis-wineman
-is-first-autistic-contestant.

CHAPTER 7—THE POWER OF ADVOCACY

1. Jesse A. Saperstein, *Getting a Life With Asperger's* (New York:
Perigee Books, 2014), 165.

2. Ron Sandison, "Challenging Waves: A Surfer Who Understands
Himself Better After Getting an Aspergers Diagnosis," Not Alone,
posted by Sandra Peters, October 17, 2014, accessed November 3, 2015,
http://specialneedsparenting.net/challenging-waves/, used with permission; Sal Ruibal, "Surfer Marzo Rides Waves of the Ocean and
Autism," *USA Today*, September 28, 2009, accessed October 30, 2015,
http://usatoday30.usatoday.com/sports/action/2009-09-27-marzo-
surfer-autism-aspergers_N.htm.

3. Ibid.

4. Ruibal, "Surfer Marzo Rides Waves of the Ocean and Autism."

5. Sandison, "Challenging Waves: A Surfer Who Understands
Himself Better after Getting an Aspergers Diagnosis."

6. Ibid.

7. Jesse A. Saperstein, *Atypical: Life With Asperger's in 20⅓ Chapters* (New York: Perigee Books, 2010), 48.

8. Melanie Jordan, "Workplace Accommodation Tips," Autism Research Institute, accessed December 15, 2015, http://autism.com /adults_accommodations2.

9. Robison, *Look Me in the Eye: My Life With Asperger's*, 194.

CHAPTER 8—ABA THERAPY

1. Kurt Norman Woeller, in communication with the author, July 17, 2014; Autism Action Plan, accessed February 5, 2016, http:// autismactionplan.com/.

2. Bobby Newman, *When Everybody Cares: Case Studies of ABA With People With Autism* (New York: AMAC, 1999), 44.

3. Albert J. Kearney, *Understanding Applied Behavior Analysis* (Philadelphia, PA: Jessica Kingsley Publishers, 2008), 68.

4. O. Ivar Lovaas, *Teaching Developmentally Disabled Children: The Me Book* (Austin, TX: PRO-ED, 1981), x.

5. For more information, see "Negative Reinforcement" at the Educate Autism website, accessed November 2, 2015, http://www .educateautism.com/behavioural-principles/negative-reinforcement .html.

6. From author's interview with Jas Dimitrion on July 3, 2014.

7. Mickey Keenan, Ken P. Kerr, and Karola Dillenburger, *Parent's Education as Autism Therapists* (Philadelphia, PA: Jessica Kingsley Publishers, 2000), 23.

8. Newman, *When Everybody Cares*, 19.

9. Brian King's Facebook blog August 4, 2014, accessed November 2, 2015, https://www.facebook.com/sozensho/posts/102042512485 06115. Used with permission.

10. From author's interview with Beth Aune on July 13, 2014.

11. Volkmar and Wiesner, *A Practical Guide to Autism*, 213–214.

12. Newman, *When Everybody Cares*, 92.

13. Linda A. Hodgdon, *Solving Behavior Problems in Autism* (Troy, MI: QuirkRoberts Publishing, 1999), 212.

CHAPTER 9—STORIES FROM THE HEART

1. You can read Buttercup's story at Lois Brady, "Some Pig! Some Impact! Buttercup!", Speech Therapy for Autism, November 13, 2012, accessed November 2, 2015, http://proactivespeech.wordpress.com /2012/11/13/some-pig-some-impact-buttercup/.

2. Kahil Gibran, "On Joy and Sorrow," *The Prophet* (New York: Alfred A. Knopf, 1923), accessed November 2, 2015, http://www.npr .org/programs/death/readings/spiritual/gibran.html.

3. As quoted in Anne Lamont, *Plan B: Further Thoughts on Faith* (New York: Riverhead Books, 2005), 39

CHAPTER 10—MY JOURNEY WITH AUTISM

1. Adapted from Ron Sandison, "My Journey as a Minister With Autism," Autism Speaks, November 11, 2014.
2. John Elder Robison, *Be Different* (New York: Broadway Paperbacks, 2011), 22.
3. Oswald Chambers, *My Utmost for His Highest* (Uhrichsville, OH: Barbour Publishing, 1935), entry for August 1.
4. Kelly Langston, *Autism's Hidden Blessings* (Grand Rapids, MI: Kregel Publications, 2009), 158.
5. K. C. King, "The Hottest Love Has the Coldest End," Philosiblogy.com, January 26, 2013, http://philosi blog.com/2013/01/26/the-hottest-love-has-the-coldest-end/.
6. As quoted in Zig Ziglar and Ike Reighard, *The One Year Daily Insights With Zig Ziglar* (Carol Stream, IL: Tyndale House, 2009).
7. From author's interview with Jill Marzo on September 21, 2014.
8. As quoted by Charles R. Swindoll, *Man to Man: Chuck Swindoll Selects His Most Significant Writings for Men* (Grand Rapids, MI: Zondervan, 1996), 138.
9. Stephen R. Covey, *The 7 Habits of Highly Effective People* (New York: Simon & Schuster, 1989), 235.

CHAPTER 11—THE FUTURE OF AUTISM—FULL CIRCLE

1. Robison, *Be Different*, 37.
2. From author's interview with Pastor Joni Parsley on September 15, 2014.
3. Carley, *Asperger's From the Inside Out*, 12.
4. Jeff Davidson, "Our Children: A Tapestry of God's Grace," Not Alone, November 14, 2014, accessed November 3, 2015, http://specialneedsparenting.net/children-tapestry-gods-grace-guest-post-jeff-davidson/.
5. This comment and others that follow come from author's interview with Edie S. Brannigan, the mother of Mikey Brannigan, on September 8, 2014.
6. From author's interview with Laura L. Corby on September 7, 2014. From author's interview with Brian R. King on June 1, 2014.
7. This and subsequent comments in this chapter came from Ron Sandison, "Small Beginnings: A Story of Insurmountable Odds," Not Alone, March 25, 2015, accessed February 5, 2016, http://

specialneedsparenting.net/small-beginnings-a-story-of-insurmount
able-odds/. Used with permission.

8. Patty Myers, "He Has What?", Not Alone, December 8, 2014, accessed November 3, 2015, http://specialneedsparenting.net/he-has -what/.

9. St. Athanasius the Great, *The Life of St. Anthony the Great* (Willits, CA: Eastern Orthodox Books), 81–83. The quoted material is my paraphrase.

APPENDIX A—UNDERSTANDING AUTISM

1. Simon Baron-Cohen, *Autism and Asperger Syndrome*, 25.

2. Picture Exchange Communication System, http://www.pecsusa .com/pecs.php.

3. National Autism Resources, http://www.nationalautism resources.com/picture-exchange-communication-sytem.html.

APPENDIX C—BIBLICAL PRINCIPLES FOR ADVOCACY

1. Brad H. Young, *Jesus the Jewish Theologian* (Peabody, MA: Hendrickson Publishers, 1995), 171.

CONNECT WITH US!

**CHARISMA
HOUSE**

(Spiritual Growth)

Facebook.com/CharismaHouse

@CharismaHouse

Instagram.com/CharismaHouseBooks

SILOAM

(Health)

Pinterest.com/CharismaHouse

REALMS

(Fiction)

Facebook.com/RealmsFiction

Ignite Your SPIRITUAL HEALTH with these FREE Newsletters

CHARISMA HEALTH
Get information and news on health-related topics and studies, and tips for healthy living.

POWER UP! FOR WOMEN
Receive encouraging teachings that will empower you for a Spirit-filled life.

CHARISMA MAGAZINE NEWSLETTER
Get top-trending articles, Christian teachings, entertainment reviews, videos and more.

CHARISMA NEWS WEEKLY
Get the latest breaking news from an evangelical perspective every Monday.

SIGN UP AT:
nl.charismamag.com

CHARISMA MEDIA